Cooking with Faith

125 CLASSIC AND HEALTHY SOUTHERN RECIPES

Faith Ford
with Melissa Clark

FOOD PHOTOGRAPHS BY MARK THOMAS

SCRIBNER
New York   London   Toronto   Sydney

SCRIBNER
1230 Avenue of the Americas
New York, NY 10020

SCRIBNER and design are trademarks of
Macmillan Library Reference USA, Inc., used under license
by Simon & Schuster, the publisher of this work.

For information about special discounts for bulk purchases,
please contact Simon & Schuster Special Sales:
1-800-456-6798 or business@simonandschuster.com

Designed by Kyoko Watanabe

Text set in Esprit

Manufactured in the United States of America

1   3   5   7   9   10   8   6   4   2

Library of Congress Control Number: 2004045285

ISBN 0-7432-5165-2

This book is dedicated to the amazing women in my family who are no longer with us: my two fearless grandmothers, Bernice Ford and Cora Walker, and my sweet aunt Katherine Ryan. They were three wonderful women, and three wonderful cooks, and I was blessed to have learned from all of them.

Acknowledgments

This book would not have been possible if not for my mother, Patricia Walker Ford, who is chiefly responsible for keeping the spirit of our family recipes alive, and inspiring me to do the same. My advice to anyone with children is to encourage them to cook the way my mom encouraged me: whenever I asked her to make something I loved, she told me, "Well, go in there and start . . . I'll talk you through it." A schoolteacher for twenty years, she always said that there's no such thing as a mistake, there's only a lesson learned for the next time—especially when it comes to cooking. Thanks for everything, Mom!

During the writing and recipe testing process, I felt so lucky to have the help and support of my family and friends, including everyone who gave me recipes and ideas for this book. This includes my sister and mentor Devon O'Day, my aunt Brenda Johnston, who keeps us on track with the facts on the family, my cousin Sue Walker, my daddy, Charles, who keeps me laughing, and of course my husband and constant companion, Campion Murphy.

I also want to thank my coauthor Melissa Clark, whose attention to detail has been amazing, and without whom this dream could not have been fulfilled.

Many thanks are due to the tireless recipe testing and editing of Karen Rush, Zoe Singer, and Sara Epstein. I'm also lucky to be able to thank my fantastic editors at Scribner, Beth Wareham and Rica Allannic, who had enough faith in the proposal to turn it into a book.

Last, but not at all least, I must send a huge heartfelt thanks to one of the biggest crusaders behind this book, and possibly the most encouraging fan of my cooking all along, Candice Bergen. She encouraged me to write this book in the first place. So anyone who enjoys a recipe from this collection really has her to thank.

CONTENTS

CHAPTER 3: *Soups, Gumbos, and Chilis*

CHAPTER 4: *Fish and Shellfish*

CHAPTER 5: *Poultry*

CHAPTER 6: *Meat*

CHAPTER 7: *Side Dishes*

CHAPTER 8: *Breakfasts, Breads, and Beverages*

CHAPTER 9: *Desserts*

CHAPTER 10: *Preserves, Pickles, and Seasonings*

When Faith and I started working on *Murphy Brown* in 1988, she was very young but she knew how to do two things: She knew how to act and she knew how to cook. As I am a die-hard eater, it was her cooking that really got my attention.

It started with her bringing home-baked, still steaming fluffy biscuits to the set or fresh peach cobbler or corn muffins. Coconut cake, blondies—things she'd made just *that morning,* still *hot* and *bubbling.* The smell would slither around the set and soon you couldn't get *near* the long crafts table (the snack zone for the crew) because it was packed with people in line for Faith's food. And not just baked goods, but black-eyed peas, jambalaya, gumbo, po' boys. Foods I'd only read about in travel magazines. Sumptuous-looking, delicious-smelling, mouthwatering, my-mama-taught-me meals.

In the mornings, on the set for breakfast, Faith would scoop out the insides of a split bagel and fill it with egg-white salad—hard-boiled egg whites mixed with Dijon mustard, dill, capers, and mayonnaise—which she'd whip up while the bagel was toasting. I would drool in my car on the way to the studio just thinking about Faith's stuffed bagel (*Bagel Farci,* as I called it) and hope she'd have time to make me one . . . or two.

Of course, if she *really* wanted to get me, her secret weapon was mini pecan pies that melted in your mouth. I swear—the *crust* was *so light* . . . and buttery . . . and they were bite-sized so you could eat about forty and not even feel full—just fat.

One rainy night, Faith and I met on a hilltop halfway between our two houses so she could hand me a crock of gumbo hot off the stove for my husband, who craved it. She'd packed it in a willow basket, lined with blue and white gingham.

Faith's food is always presented wonderfully: colors of containers coordinate with the napkins they're nestled in, Mason jars are tied with French ribbon. When she serves food, she always does it beautifully—the table looking as festive as the meal. Her kitchen is comfy and cozy with overstuffed sofas, a collection of ceramic roosters, bowls heaping with tomatoes from her garden. Attention is given to every detail.

Of course, Faith is a fast learner and in the early "Murphy" years, besides comedy and cuisine, she developed expertise in how to dress and how to decorate a house, talents she already possessed but now had the means to express.

During our ten years on *Murphy Brown,* I came to depend upon Faith's advice for virtually everything: "Faithy, what should I have for lunch?" "Fa-ayth. Do I look too fat in this dress?" "Fa-ayyth, do I put a lamp here or a mirror?" "Faithy, what do you think of the color of this wall?" "How do you keep the birds off your tomatoes?" "Who can I get to cut my hair?" "*Should* I cut my hair?" "How come I'm not getting a laugh with this line?"

Everything Faith does, she does well. I think it's a combination of natural ability, Southern pride, and a mama who taught her how to plant and pot and pickle and pluck, and a daddy who taught her how to shoot whatever moves in that swamp where they had their huntin' camp.

In fact, *Cooking with Faith* is just the beginning of what I think should be a series: *Decorating with Faith, Gardening with Faith, Dressing with Faith, Exercising with Faith, Dieting with Faith,* and, my personal favorite, *Eating with Faith*—which I hope to do more of now that she's been considerate enough to move to New York to star in a series. We'll start with the mini pecan pies. . . .

—*Candice Bergen*

COOKING WITH FAITH

Introduction

When people first meet me, they think it's a novel idea that I'm an actress who cooks. But I've been cooking for longer than I've been acting. Growing up in the small town of Pineville, Louisiana, I was the shy and scrawny kid (even though I ate like a pig) who disappeared into the wall. Since I wasn't particularly outgoing, I guess I found my way to popularity by learning to cook at a young age. People always like someone who bakes a killer brownie, or invites you over for a homemade meal.

I learned how to make my first recipe when I was about eight years old. It was purple hull peas, cooked until they're soft with a little bit of bacon. If you've never had them, purple hull peas are related to black-eyed peas but the pea is greener. My maternal grandparents, Larry and Cora Walker, grew them on their farm, and my grandma Cora and my mother, Pat Ford, made them for me ever since I was a baby. So I loved them from when I was old enough to chew (or even before—my mother says she craved them when she was pregnant with me!). But there was one thing I always noticed: my grandmother made hers a little bit better than my mother did.

One summer when my sister and I came home after spending a couple of weeks with my grandma Cora, I said, "Mama, I think you need a new stove." When she asked why, I said, "Well, your stove just doesn't cook purple hull peas like Grandma Cora's stove."

My mother laughed. "Well," she said, "I don't think it's the stove. I think it's the way Grandma Cora makes those peas. I tell you what, the next time you go over to Grandma Cora's, I want you to watch her like a hawk. And when you come home you can be in charge of making the peas from now on. So you have to learn how to make them just like she makes them."

And I did.

That's how it started. I discovered that I loved to cook, and that I was good at it, too. As a teenager I would spend hours watching Julia Child and her local Pineville equivalent, Mildred Swift, on television. I was fascinated by the way Julia kind of bumbled around until she came up with something great. I could relate. For me cooking was always about finding my way in the kitchen, trying out new ideas until I found one that worked. Then it became part of my repertoire.

But even before all that, I had learned the basics from my mother and grandmother, like how to assemble your ingredients and do the prep work before you start cooking. My grandmother was an amazing cook and my mother and her sister, my aunt Brenda, still are. Not that they would cook anything fancy, just good, old-fashioned, homey food—

Southern-style, naturally, since we lived in the South. They didn't use written recipes, they simply cooked from their souls.

In addition to giving me their vintage recipes, my mother and grandmother taught me about all the little details and techniques that go not just into making a dish, but into making it special. Even toast could be special. I make toast the way my grandma used to. She never had a pop-up toaster, so she'd use a toaster oven or broiler, toast the bread a little bit, spread butter on it, and put it back in, so that when you took it out it had little pools of butter on the top. It's amazing toast. To this day only a toaster oven or broiler will do for me. That same care and attention makes everything a little more delicious, even if it's as simple as spreading the mayonnaise out to the corners of the crust when you make a sandwich, or standing and stirring, not walking off, when you make brown gravy.

Another thing I learned from my family was how to eat balanced, healthful meals. This may surprise you if you think that all Southern cooking is heavy and fat-and-carbohydrate based. And while we certainly ate plenty of the traditional dishes like chicken and dumplings, roast beef po' boys, gumbo with andouille sausages, and all those heavenly Southern desserts like pecan pie and banana pudding, we also loved vegetables, and made them a large part of every meal.

My grandma and grandpa Walker had a farm and my parents a garden, so we grew our own mustard and turnip greens, squash, cabbage, peas, okra, and tomatoes. There was little we didn't grow. My dad, Charles, and his parents, Grandpa Dewey and Grandma Bernice Ford, grew a special kind of speckled green beans—Grandpa Ford was so proud of those. We always had fresh corn from my Grandpa Walker's farm—we helped harvest it each year. And there were so many purple hull peas that my sister and I would stain our fingers lilac having pea-shelling contests. Whoever won got a nickel or an extra dessert, which seemed like a big haul at the time!

In the heart of summer, our meals were based around our home-grown fruits and vegetables. With breakfast biscuits there were homemade fig preserves with figs from Grandma Walker's three huge fig trees, and peaches from her peach trees. At lunch we'd have purple hull peas, of course, and greens simmered until falling-apart tender, creamed corn, fried okra, cornbread, and fresh sliced tomatoes, with peach ice cream for dessert. I never forgot the way those tomatoes tasted. It's the kind of thing you hang on to.

All of it is. Once you know what it's like to eat meals made with love and care, and plenty of homegrown fresh fruits and vegetables, you'll find a way to keep doing it.

I did, even when I moved to New York City at the age of seventeen. I moved there to model for the summer and make money for school, but it didn't work out that way. I ended up taking acting classes and working commercially, and, at the same time, cooking more than ever. Auditioning and running around the city can wear you down, and I would find myself coming home from a stressful day and chopping vegetables. The meditative aspects of cooking helped me relax. It was comforting. So I'd cook up a beef stew or a big vegetable soup or pot of greens. I don't know who I thought was going to eat all that food, and I'd end up feeding all my roommates and inviting friends over. Sharing food is a great way to create bonds with people.

In New York I was exposed to a lot of other influences when I went out to eat. We never really went to restaurants when I was growing up. Sure, there was barbecue and pizza and things like that. But going out to dinner in New York opened my eyes. If I had a dish I liked at a restaurant, I would try to memorize its flavors and re-create it at home. I still do that today.

After four years in New York, I moved to Los Angeles and continued working and taking acting classes, and cooking, of course. I would use my cooking skills to bribe people to come over to my house to rehearse so I didn't have to schlep out to theirs. I also would cater our showcases—where we would perform for agents, managers, and casting directors. I guess I thought if I didn't get an acting job I could get some kind of cooking job from it. But eventually, I did get an acting job—the role of Corky on *Murphy Brown*.

For me, working steadily didn't mean giving up cooking. I'd make food for people on the set all the time. I would prepare my breakfast—maybe a scooped-out bagel filled with egg white salad and tomatoes—and when I sat down to read through the script Candice Bergen would say, "Well, that looks really good. Can I have one?" So I would make her one, too. Once on the set of a movie I even found myself in the catering truck, teaching the caterer to make a giant pot of authentic Louisiana gumbo! Food and cooking may not have been part of the script, but they were always on my mind.

It was in Los Angeles that my own cooking style started to develop. That's when I began experimenting, and making the traditional recipes I grew up with a little lighter. As an actress, I had to keep fit. I started using olive oil in things instead of lard or bacon, just to see what would happen. That's how I adapted my mother's Sizzlin' Salad (page 31). She always made it with bacon grease, which is delicious. But I thought, what if I try making this with olive oil? And it worked! That was just the beginning.

But always, at the heart of my cooking style are my mother and grandmother's treasured dishes. I never go long without making something of theirs. But I also continue to update and lighten them so they fit into my lifestyle in Los Angeles. It's probably in part because of the culture I live in now, but I find that I care more each day about what I put into my body. Striving to eat healthfully means keeping my cooking really clean, simple, and natural.

I don't go overboard. As with my family's meals during my childhood, balance is what I look for. Let's face it, if I'm going to have fried catfish, I'm going to have fried catfish. Sometimes I'll make oven-fried catfish, which is less messy and a little healthier, but there are times when only deep-fried catfish will do. So I'll serve it on a bed of greens and to me, the vegetables balance the meal. And maybe I'll eat a little less catfish because the greens filled me up. It's a real change from the all-you-can-eat catfish places I went to as a kid, where the fried fish was served with hush puppies and potato logs and then you might have a little bit of coleslaw and some pickles. I do things differently now.

Whenever I can, I make healthy substitutions, and I always try to use fresh ingredients. I don't cook my greens to death anymore like we used to. It takes eight to ten minutes to cook mustard and turnip greens, whereas we used to cook them for hours. And we used salt pork. Now I rely on turkey sausage, turkey bacon, and turkey tasso. Where I can, I cook with olive oil or vegetable oil instead of lard, and add butter as a flavoring at the end of cooking.

All of this keeps my cooking a little bit more healthful, but still fulfilling and delicious.

And that is the philosophy behind *Cooking with Faith*.

This book is about the way I cook now—a combination of the homespun, heirloom dishes I grew up with, and my own lighter, healthier, more modern versions and creations. It's also about the relationships in my family, as I've cooked and adapted family recipes. We continue to learn from each other in the kitchen and my mom shares her opinions in the "Mom Says" notes throughout the book. There is food here for anyone, and anytime, whether you feel like making my grandmother's fabulous peach cobbler, my mother's meat loaf with brown mushroom gravy, or my warm chicken salad with field greens and hot-and-sweet pecans. I want to encourage daughters who might not cook to try to with their mom or their mom's mom. I think women have so much to gain from cooking together, especially moms and daughters.

But as much as it's about what I love to cook, *Cooking with Faith* is also about helping others tap into a way of cooking that is simple yet full of flavor and feeling. This kind of cooking is timely because we've gotten away from the traditions that I learned growing up. Well-made food is an experience. It's about taking pride in what you eat. It's a remedy for an increasingly fast food–reliant society—I mean, how can you be that much in a hurry?

As I've learned through the years, meals don't need to be extravagant, just made with love. I hope this book shows people that even basic, homey food is excellent if you pay attention to details. Cooking and sharing my recipes is a way of preserving something that was important to me in my formative years, something that I know every cook will understand. It's not the fanciest cooking in the world, but whether it's a steaming bowl of grits, a crisp salmon cake, or a fluffy slice of lemon pie, it tastes so much better—and means so much more—when you take the time and the care to do it right.

CHAPTER 1

Appetizers, Snacks, and Sandwiches

Chilled Sugar Snap Peas with Honey-Soy Dipping Sauce

Sugar snaps grow well in Louisiana, and I love to just sit and eat them like potato chips. I boil up a bunch for a minute or two, then stick them in the fridge, ready to pull out as an hors d'oeuvre for guests to nibble on while I'm cooking.

The dipping sauce is salty like ponzu sauce—which I order with edamame, or fresh soybeans, when we go out for sushi—but with a little honey for Southern sweetness and hot sauce for zing. It's also great as an alternative dip for Crispy Chicken Tenders (page 22) or with other veggies like carrots, steamed broccoli, and cucumbers.

SERVES 6

Salt
¼ cup soy sauce
¼ cup rice vinegar
2 tablespoons finely chopped fresh ginger
2 tablespoons honey
¼ teaspoon hot sauce
1 garlic clove, minced or passed through a garlic press
2 tablespoons Asian sesame oil or toasted sesame oil
1 tablespoon vegetable oil
2 scallions, chopped
1 pound sugar snap peas, trimmed

1. Bring a saucepan of salted water to a boil and fill a large bowl with water and ice.
2. In a stand blender, process the soy sauce, vinegar, ginger, honey, hot sauce, and garlic until smooth. With the motor running, slowly drizzle in the oils. Transfer to a small bowl and stir in the scallions.
3. Blanch the sugar snaps in the boiling water for 1½ to 2 minutes, then drain and immediately transfer to the ice water to stop the cooking. Drain well and serve the peas with the sauce as a dip. The peas and sauce can be made up to 2 days ahead. Store, covered, in the refrigerator.

Artichoke-Parmesan Dip

The first time I had artichoke dip was when a guy I dated in high school took me to a party where there was a bowl of it. I remember thinking, "This is the most amazing food." "Oh, honey, we've been doing this for years!" my friends said. But it was news to me. I still feel I missed out, and I may be overcompensating, dressing up my dip with fresh basil and Cajun seasonings, but it's just so good. I make it much lighter than traditional dip, so it's more about the artichokes and herbs.

MAKES ABOUT 2 CUPS, SERVING 8

½ cup plain dried bread crumbs
2 tablespoons butter, melted
2 (6-ounce) jars marinated artichoke hearts, drained
4 garlic cloves, minced or passed through a garlic press
1 cup regular or nonfat cottage cheese
1 cup grated Parmesan cheese
⅓ cup chopped fresh basil
3 tablespoons light or regular mayonnaise
1 tablespoon freshly squeezed lemon juice (from about ½ lemon)
1 teaspoon Faith's Special Seasoning (page 266) or
   Cajun seasoning (see Sources, page 267)
1 teaspoon hot sauce
Crackers or bread

1. In a small bowl, combine the bread crumbs and melted butter. Set aside.
2. In a food processor, or on a large cutting board, chop the artichokes and garlic together until the artichokes are coarsely chopped and the mixture is a little chunky.
3. In a medium bowl, combine the artichoke mixture, cottage cheese, Parmesan, basil, mayonnaise, lemon juice, Faith's seasoning, and hot sauce and mix well. Transfer the mixture to an 8-inch baking dish (or similar sized dish) and smooth the surface. This can be done up to 6 hours ahead. Refrigerate, covered, until ready to bake.
4. Preheat the oven to 375 degrees F.
5. Top the dip with the bread crumb mixture and bake for 25 to 30 minutes, until bubbly and golden brown. Serve hot with crackers or bread for dipping.

Sweet and Spicy Skillet-Toasted Pecans

I like to set out little bowls of these crispy pecans for people to nibble on with drinks at parties. They're really quite addictive. They're also great on salads. Little packages of these also make nice homemade gifts for the holidays, and the recipe can be doubled easily.

MAKES 2 CUPS

> 2 cups pecans
> 2 tablespoons butter
> ¼ cup honey
> 4 teaspoons Faith's Special Seasoning (page 266) or
>   Cajun seasoning (see Sources, page 267)

1. In a nonstick skillet over medium-high heat, toast the pecans for 2 minutes, tossing occasionally, until fragrant.
2. Add the butter and toss it with the pecans until it melts. Turn off the heat and add the honey and Faith's seasoning. Stir to coat well and spread out in a single layer on wax paper to cool. The pecans will keep at room temperature in an airtight container for up to 1 month.

Perfect-for-a-Potluck
Deviled Eggs

You rarely go to a potluck luncheon or family get-together in the South where you don't see deviled eggs. And you might think a deviled egg is just a deviled egg, but everybody makes them differently. I've always loved my mom's so much that when I was little, she'd make a couple extra for me to have on our way to the party.

MAKES 1 DOZEN

6 eggs, hard-boiled (see Boiling Eggs), peeled and halved lengthwise
3 tablespoons light or regular mayonnaise
1 tablespoon chopped pimento
1 tablespoon sweet pickle relish or chopped dill pickle (whichever you prefer)
1 tablespoon chopped green olives
1 tablespoon chopped scallion (green part only)
Salt and black pepper
Sweet paprika

> ## BOILING EGGS
>
> Choose a saucepan large enough to hold the eggs in a single layer. Place the eggs in the saucepan and fill with enough water to cover them by 1 inch. Bring up to a boil, then start timing and boil for 1 minute. Cover the pan, turn off the heat, and let rest for 15 minutes. It's easiest to peel hard-boiled eggs under a stream of cold water. The fresher the eggs, the more difficult they are to peel.

1. Scoop out the yolks from the eggs and place them in a bowl. Arrange the whites on a serving plate and set aside. Mash the yolks well with a fork, then add the mayonnaise, pimento, pickle, olives, scallion, and salt and pepper.
2. Spoon the mixture into the egg white shells and dust lightly with paprika. The pretty reds and greens should peek through. Deviled eggs can be prepared up to 6 hours ahead. Store them, covered, in the refrigerator.

Po' Boys at Ray's Pee Gee

Po' boys are a big thing all over the South—I would be willing to bet there's not a person in Louisiana who doesn't eat them once or more a week. You can basically make anything into a po' boy, so you never get sick of them. They're the South's answer to a hero sandwich, grilled, on French bread. You grill the inside of the bread and fill it with hot or room-temperature ingredients like sliced roast beef or turkey or fried fish, oysters, or shrimp, and then you can either eat it as is or grill and press the whole sandwich. Most po' boy places give you a choice of pressed or unpressed. Both are great.

The best place for po' boys, ever, as far as I'm concerned, is Ray's Pee Gee in Monroe, Louisiana. That's where my family went on Friday nights when I was growing up, and for us, Ray's po' boys set the gold standard.

PO' BOY WISDOM

It's not hard to make a great po' boy, but there are some things to keep in mind. One of the most important is the bread. You've got to find a soft, light loaf of French or Italian bread that's not too dense or crusty. The loaf should be about 18 inches long, with a tender crust that you can easily bite through and an airy inside to soak up the butter. Don't use a fine French baguette or a chewy Italian loaf from a fancy bakery. Those are better for eating by themselves. I always say that if a loaf of bread is really good to eat by itself without being heated in plenty of butter, it's probably not the right kind for a po' boy.

And another thing: you have to use a griddle or a frying pan or even an electric pancake pan—something with a flat surface—to toast just the insides of the bread. Don't use a toaster oven because it will dry out the tops and cause the bread to crumble when you bite it.

When you dress the bread, make sure to spread the mayonnaise to the edges so you get some in every mouthful. And be sure to have all your fixings for the sandwich ready before you grill the bread. That way, when it's done, you can put the sandwich together quickly and serve it while still hot.

That's a po' boy at its best!

Of course, you can get a po' boy anywhere in Louisiana now, and even across the country, but they're not the same. They don't dress them right, with mayonnaise and pickles, or take the time to make sure the bread is hot, buttery, and crispy. At Ray's, they'd always have a big metal pan of melted butter that they'd brush on the inside of the bread. Then the slices went face down onto the griddle until they turned golden brown and were heated all the way through. Their po' boys were served fresh and hot, so they stayed juicy and crunchy at the same time.

When I was eight, my family moved to Pineville, about two hours away from Monroe. But we still craved Ray's po' boys and would drive there every now and again for dinner. After a while, my mother said, "This is ridiculous, to drive so far for a sandwich. I'm going to learn how to make them at home." And she did, following Ray's example; then she taught me. It's not quite Ray's, but I think our version is a pretty close second.

⚜ **Mom Says:** The sandwiches can be kept in a warm oven (preheat it to 250 degrees F, then turn off the heat) for 5 or 10 minutes if there is any waiting for everyone to get to the table. These recipes make two po' boys each. Most people consider a half loaf of bread to be one whole po' boy. So, a fourth of a loaf is half a sandwich. At most places, you can order either a half or a whole. A hungry man can usually eat a whole one. Faith's husband can, and then will exercise two hours in the gym just to work it off. But Faith and I will usually just eat a half.

Rest of the Pot Roast
Po' Boys

Roast beef po' boys were always my favorite at Ray's Pee Gee's, and they're a perfect lunch or supper for the day after you make pot roast. In fact, my real reason for making a beef pot roast is so I can have a po' boy the next day! I like mine with a little horseradish, but of course the amount of heat is up to you.

    Mom Says: Some po' boys are good when only the inside of the bread is toasted. But there's just something about a roast beef po' boy that you're going to dip in gravy. It's much better when you press and grill the outside for a minute after the whole thing is put together.

SERVES 2 TO 4

> 1 pound roast beef (see Juicy Beef Pot Roast, page 134), thinly sliced
> 1 cup gravy from Juicy Beef Pot Roast
> ¼ cup light or regular mayonnaise
> 2 tablespoons bottled horseradish, optional
> 1 large soft loaf French or Italian bread, sliced in half crosswise and
>   lengthwise (see Po' Boy Wisdom, page 10)
> 6 tablespoons butter, melted
> 2 large tomatoes, sliced
> 4 large romaine lettuce leaves, shredded

1. To heat the meat, warm the gravy in a skillet and then place the meat in it, a few slices at a time, for 3 to 4 minutes each. (Alternatively, you can steam the slices in a steamer insert in a large covered pot for 3 to 4 minutes.)
2. In a small bowl, combine the mayonnaise with the horseradish, if using.
3. Warm a griddle or skillet over medium-high heat. Have all the other ingredients laid out so you're ready to assemble sandwiches as soon as the bread is done. Brush the cut side of each piece of bread with melted butter. Place the bread slices buttered side down and cook until browned, 2 to 3 minutes.

4. Liberally spread each slice of bread with mayonnaise. Layer the bottom halves of the bread with sliced tomatoes, shredded lettuce, and slices of the warm beef. Close the sandwiches and return them to the warm griddle for 1 minute. Press down firmly and cut in half on a cutting board. Serve immediately, with individual dipping bowls of gravy for each person.

Me and my mom, Pat, fixing dinner in the kitchen.

Catfish Po' Boys with Creole Tartar Sauce

In the South, whenever you do a fish fry, you should always offer pickles on the side. If you also put out some freshly grilled bread, then anyone who wants a po' boy can make it right then and there. When it comes to a fried fish po' boy, that's when you get into your tartar sauces instead of using plain mayonnaise. For this recipe, I make a spiced up dressing that I call Creole tartar sauce because when you order something "Creole" in New Orleans, like a Creole Bloody Mary, it's just loaded with horseradish. And so is the sauce.

These po' boys start out with Southern-Style Fried Catfish. You can assemble them using lettuce and tomatoes, and serve a big scoop of Grandpa Walker's Favorite Crunchy Southern Slaw on the side. But what I really like to do is to leave off the lettuce and tomato altogether and spread the slaw right on top of the fish inside the sandwich instead. It adds a great crunch.

SERVES 2 TO 4

Creole Tartar Sauce

> ¼ cup light or regular mayonnaise
> 2 tablespoons catsup
> Freshly squeezed juice of ¼ lemon
> 1½ teaspoons bottled horseradish
> 1½ teaspoons sweet pickle relish
> ½ teaspoon hot sauce
> ¼ teaspoon Worcestershire sauce

In a small bowl, whisk together all the ingredients. Refrigerate, covered, until ready to use, or overnight.

Po' Boys

> 1 soft loaf French or Italian bread, sliced in half crosswise and
>   lengthwise (see Po' Boy Wisdom, page 10)
> 6 tablespoons butter, melted
> 1 pound catfish fillets, fried (see Southern-Style Fried Catfish, page 82)
> 4 large lettuce leaves
> 2 large tomatoes, sliced
> 1 recipe Grandpa Walker's Favorite Crunchy Southern Slaw (page 38), optional
> Sliced dill pickles

1. Warm a griddle or skillet over medium-high heat. Have all the ingredients laid out so you're ready to assemble sandwiches as soon as the bread is done. Brush the cut side of each piece of bread with melted butter. Place the bread slices buttered side down and cook until browned, 2 to 3 minutes.

2. Liberally spread both sides of the bread with the Creole Tartar Sauce. Place a piece of warm fried catfish on top of a slice of bread, followed by lettuce and tomato (or a scoop of coleslaw, if using), then sliced pickles. Place the other half of the bread on top, press firmly, cut in half, and serve immediately, with extra tartar sauce on the side.

Smoked Turkey and Avocado Po' Boys with Sweet Tangy Mayo

This is not your typical Louisiana po' boy. No one there would ever think to add slices of avocado. But in L.A., avocados are used everywhere, and I love them. However, there's an art to using one in a po' boy. You have to press the avocado onto the bread and compact it a little so that it doesn't slide off the sandwich. If you use the avocado next to the tomato and lettuce, it slips right out the sides when you bite down. But if you put it between the bread and the turkey, it will stay put—until you eat it up, that is.

SERVES 2 TO 4

Sweet Tangy Mayo
> ½ cup light or regular mayonnaise
> ¼ cup catsup
> ¼ cup sweet pickle relish
> 1 teaspoon hot sauce

Mix together all the ingredients, cover, and refrigerate until ready to use, or overnight.

Po' Boys
> 2 tablespoons olive oil
> ¾ pound sliced smoked turkey breast
> 1 large soft loaf French or Italian bread, sliced in half crosswise and lengthwise (see Po' Boy Wisdom, page 10)
> 6 tablespoons butter, melted
> 1 large avocado, peeled and sliced
> 4 large red leaf lettuce leaves, shredded
> 2 large tomatoes, sliced

1. In a large skillet, warm the olive oil over medium-high heat. Fold the turkey slices in half and fit as many in the skillet as you can. Sear the slices for about 30 seconds on each side, then transfer them to a plate lined with a paper towel. Repeat until all the

slices are seared. Turn off the heat, return all the turkey slices to the skillet, and cover to keep warm.

2. Warm a griddle or skillet over medium-high heat. Have all the ingredients laid out so you're ready to assemble sandwiches as soon as the bread is done. Brush the cut side of each piece of bread with melted butter. Place the bread slices buttered side down and cook until browned, 2 to 3 minutes.

3. Liberally spread each slice of the warm bread with tangy mayo. On the bottom halves of the bread, layer the avocado, turkey, lettuce, and tomato, in that order. Place the warm top halves on each sandwich, press firmly, cut in half, and serve immediately.

Grilled Veggie Po' Boys with Homespun Basil Hummus

Putting hummus on a po' boy with grilled veggies is a terrific idea, though not very traditional in the South. I like it because chickpeas are full of protein and really fill you up. I usually offer these po' boys as a meatless alternative at my barbecues. After everything is set out, I coach my friends on how to spread hummus on one side of the bread and layer the vegetables on top, then put a little more hummus on top of the vegetables. The flavors are amazing, and the vegetables are very juicy, so when you bite into a veggie po' boy, juice drips down the bread.

SERVES 2 TO 4

Homespun Basil Hummus

> 2 garlic cloves
> 1 (16-ounce) can chickpeas, rinsed and drained
> 3 to 4 tablespoons freshly squeezed lemon juice (from 1 lemon), to taste
> 3 tablespoons tahini
> 1 tablespoon extra-virgin olive oil
> 1 teaspoon hot sauce
> ¼ teaspoon salt
> ¼ cup chopped fresh basil

Put the garlic cloves in a food processor or blender and process or blend to finely chop. Add all the other ingredients except the basil and blend or pulse until the mixture is pureed. Add the basil and 2 tablespoons water and pulse until a spreadable consistency is achieved, adding an additional tablespoon of water if necessary. Taste and correct the seasonings, adding more lemon juice, hot sauce, and salt as needed. Refrigerate for up to 2 days or use immediately on grilled veggie po' boys.

Po' Boys

> 1 small eggplant, cut lengthwise into ¼-inch-thick slices
>
> 1 red bell pepper, cut lengthwise into ¼-inch-thick slices
>
> 2 yellow squash, cut lengthwise into ¼-inch-thick slices
>
> 3 large portobello mushrooms, cut into ¼-inch-thick slices
>
> 6 tablespoons olive oil
>
> 2 teaspoons Faith's Special Seasoning (page 266) or
>
>   Cajun seasoning (see Sources, page 267)
>
> 1 soft loaf French or Italian bread, sliced in half crosswise and
>
>   lengthwise (see Po' Boy Wisdom, page 10)

1. Preheat the grill or use a stovetop grill. Alternatively, preheat the oven to 425 degrees F.
2. Place the vegetables in a large bowl, drizzle them with 3 tablespoons of the olive oil, and sprinkle them with Faith's seasoning. Toss well.
3. Grill the vegetables, using a grilling basket if desired, turning every 5 minutes and moving them around the grill, taking care that they don't burn, until sear marks appear and they are cooked through, 10 to 15 minutes. Transfer to a platter and keep warm. If you are using the oven instead of a grill, spread the vegetables in a single layer on a baking sheet and roast in the oven until golden and tender, 20 to 25 minutes, turning once or twice to ensure even cooking.
4. Brush the cut sides of each piece of bread with the remaining 3 tablespoons oil. Place the bread slices oiled side down on the grill and cook until browned, 2 to 3 minutes.
5. Liberally spread each piece of bread with hummus. Layer veggies on each bottom slice and close with a top slice. Cut each po' boy in half and serve immediately while hot and crispy.

My Favorite Chicken Salad Sandwich with Roasted Red Peppers on Sourdough Toast

My mother used to make chicken salad with eggs and celery and finely chopped chicken, and that's a homey thing for me. I make mine a little chunkier, and I'll toss in anything from walnuts, mustard, or a little curry, to capers or gherkins. This is a very adaptable recipe. If I have extra pesto around, I spread some on the toast, and I may add fresh herbs or greens like basil or arugula to the salad. The only things I rarely change are the roasted red peppers and the bread. Really good marinated roasted red peppers are something I keep in my pantry for those times when you open the refrigerator and think, "Oh, gosh, what am I going to make a sandwich with?" They brighten up everything, from pasta to salads to sandwiches.

SERVES 8

2 cups chopped cooked chicken (see Mom Says, page 102)

2 celery stalks, chopped

½ small red onion, chopped

1 carrot, chopped

¼ cup chopped toasted pecans (see page 244)

1 tablespoon chopped fresh parsley

1 tablespoon chopped fresh cilantro

½ cup light or regular mayonnaise

¼ cup sweet pickle relish

2 tablespoons freshly squeezed lime juice (from about ½ lime)

1 tablespoon Dijon mustard

¼ teaspoon black pepper

Salt

8 slices sourdough bread

2 roasted red bell peppers, homemade or store-bought (see Roasting Peppers, opposite), seeded and halved lengthwise

2 cups watercress or shredded red leaf lettuce

1. In a medium bowl, mix together the chicken, celery, onion, carrot, pecans, parsley, and cilantro. In a separate small bowl, stir together the mayonnaise, pickle relish, lime juice, mustard, and pepper. Pour the dressing over the chicken mixture and toss thoroughly. Taste and add salt if you like. The chicken salad can be made 1 day ahead. Store it, covered, in the refrigerator.
2. Toast the bread slices. Place ½ to ⅔ cup of chicken salad on each sandwich. Put half a roasted pepper on top of the chicken salad, followed by watercress or lettuce. Place the other slice of toast on top, press each sandwich together firmly, cut in half, and serve.

ROASTING PEPPERS

I like things that are char-grilled and smoky, and peppers, both bell and chile, are no exception. Store-bought roasted peppers don't usually taste as good: You have to make sure they've been roasted (if you buy them in jars, the label will tell you if they've been roasted or not). You also should see little blackened bits of skin. Sometimes I roast or grill a bunch of peppers on the weekend, then store them in the fridge to use during the week. They also freeze well for a few weeks.

To roast the peppers, use tongs to place them directly in the flame on a gas stove burner or over the grill and keep turning until they are blackened all over and beginning to go limp. Remove each pepper from the heat, wrap it in two paper towels, and set it aside for a few minutes. As you unwrap each pepper, wipe the blackened skin off with the paper towels. Remove the seeds and stems and you're ready to go.

Crispy Chicken Tenders with Honey-Mustard Dipping Sauce

Growing up, we'd never waste a whole bunch of chickens just to have tenders made from strips of boneless skinless breasts. And when we ate chicken, it was almost always fried. But now you can buy tenders at the supermarket, and when my friends bring their kids over to the house, it's good to have things for them to eat. This appetizer is great, because people of all ages love it. If you are serving these to kids, leave out the hot sauce and substitute regular mustard for the Creole, or offer catsup on the side.

SERVES 8

Chicken Tenders
> 1 pound chicken tenders, or 1 pound chicken cutlets, cut into 1½-inch strips
> 2 tablespoons soy sauce
> 2 garlic cloves, minced or passed through a garlic press
> ½ teaspoon hot sauce, optional

1. Rinse the chicken tenders and pat dry with paper towels.
2. In a small bowl, combine the soy sauce, garlic, and hot sauce. Place the chicken in a shallow dish and pour the sauce over it. Let marinate, covered, in the refrigerator for at least an hour, or overnight.

Honey-Mustard Dipping Sauce
> 6 tablespoons olive oil
> 3 tablespoons Asian sesame oil or toasted sesame oil
> 2 tablespoons Creole mustard (see Note, opposite) or spicy brown mustard
> 2 tablespoons honey
> 2 tablespoons cider vinegar
> 2 teaspoons hot sauce, or to taste, optional
> 2 teaspoons soy sauce
> 2 garlic cloves, minced or passed through a garlic press
> Salt and black pepper to taste

Combine all the ingredients in a blender or food processor and blend or process until smooth. This sauce can be made up to 2 days in advance and kept, covered, in the refrigerator. Bring to room temperature before serving.

Coating Mix

> 1 cup cornflake crumbs
> ½ cup plain dried bread crumbs
> ½ cup Grape-Nuts cereal
> 2 tablespoons Faith's Special Seasoning (page 266) or
>   Cajun seasoning (see Sources, page 267)
> 2 large egg whites
> 1 teaspoon Creole mustard (see Note) or spicy brown mustard
> Olive oil, for brushing or spraying

1. Preheat the oven to 450 degrees F.
2. In a wide shallow bowl, mix together the cornflake crumbs, bread crumbs, Grape-Nuts, and Faith's seasoning. In another wide shallow bowl, mix together the egg whites and mustard.
3. Spray or brush a baking sheet lightly with olive oil. Dip each tender in the egg white mix, then roll it in the crumb mix and place it on the prepared baking sheet. Spray or drizzle the coated tenders with olive oil and bake for 5 minutes. Spray or drizzle them with olive oil again, then continue to bake until browned and cooked through, about 15 minutes more. Serve immediately, with the dipping sauce on the side.

NOTE: Creole mustard is more pungent than regular mustard. It's made with brown mustard seeds soaked in vinegar before being ground. If you can't find any, substitute any whole-grain spicy brown mustard.

Fried Mini Meat Pies

I love these cute little pies, which are gone in two bites. They are great for a party, and everyone will gobble them up. But these turnovers don't have to be fried to be good—there's a healthier alternative. If you prefer, place them on an oiled baking sheet, brush the tops with oil, and bake in a preheated 400 degree F oven until golden, about 15 minutes.

MAKES 24 MINI PIES

Meat Filling
> 1½ teaspoons olive oil
> 1 small onion, chopped
> ½ pound lean ground beef or ground turkey
> 2 tablespoons all-purpose flour
> ½ teaspoon salt
> ½ teaspoon chopped fresh sage
> ½ teaspoon sweet paprika
> ¼ teaspoon black pepper
> ¼ teaspoon crushed red pepper flakes
> ⅛ teaspoon cayenne pepper

1. Warm the olive oil in a heavy skillet over medium-high heat. Add the onion and ground beef or turkey and sauté, breaking up the meat as you stir, until it loses its red color, about 5 minutes.
2. Add the flour and seasonings and cook, stirring constantly, until the mixture begins to brown, 5 to 10 minutes. Set aside to cool while making the crusts. The filling can be made up to 2 days ahead. Cover and store it in the refrigerator, then bring it to room temperature before using.

Pastry
> 2 cups self-rising flour (see Note, page 192)
> ⅓ cup solid vegetable shortening
> ½ teaspoon salt
> ½ cup milk
> 1 large egg

1. Place the flour, shortening, and salt in a food processor and pulse 5 or 6 times until the mixture forms pea-sized crumbs (alternatively, cut the ingredients together in a large bowl, using a pastry cutter or two knives). In a small bowl, whisk together the milk and egg and add to the flour mixture 2 tablespoons at a time, pulsing (or mixing with a fork) after each addition until a dough forms. Do not overmix.
2. Divide the dough into thirds and roll out each piece between layers of wax paper to a ⅛-inch thickness. Using a cookie cutter or the rim of a glass, cut out 3-inch circles of dough and place them on a cookie sheet lined with wax paper, using more wax paper to separate the layers. Re-roll the scraps as necessary to make about 24 rounds. Stack the rounds in layers separated by wax paper until ready to make pies. The rounds can be covered and chilled for up to 1 day, or frozen, well wrapped, for up to 1 month.
3. Place 1 scant teaspoon of the meat mixture on each circle of dough, fold the dough in half, and seal the edges with the tines of a fork. Set aside until all the circles are filled. Or refrigerate them between layers of wax paper (and make sure to cover the top layer of pies) for up to 8 hours before frying.

To Cook
Vegetable oil

1. Fill a large heavy pan with 2 inches of vegetable oil and heat the oil to 350 degrees F (or use a deep-fryer).
2. Fry the pies, several at a time, until golden brown on both sides, 2 to 3 minutes. Transfer to a baking sheet or platter layered with paper towels and let drain briefly. Sprinkle with salt before serving if you like. Serve immediately, or keep warm in a 200 degree F oven for no more than 15 minutes.

Baked Cajun Chicken Pies

Here's another recipe for adorable little pies. Baked rather than fried, they are stuffed with chicken and sage. If you have any filling left over, it's great scrambled up in eggs or fried like a sausage patty.

MAKES ABOUT 40 MINI PIES

Pastry

 3 cups all-purpose flour, plus some for sprinkling
 1¼ cups (2 sticks plus 2 tablespoons) unsalted butter
 1½ teaspoons salt
 1 teaspoon fresh thyme, optional
 1 large egg

1. Place the flour, butter, salt, and thyme in a food processor and pulse 5 or 6 times until the mixture forms pea-sized crumbs (alternatively, cut the ingredients together in a large bowl, using a pastry cutter or two knives). Whisk together ¼ cup cold water and the egg and add this to the flour mixture 2 tablespoons at a time, pulsing (or mixing with a fork) after each addition until a dough forms. Do not overmix.
2. Turn the dough out onto a sheet of plastic wrap and shape it into a disc. Wrap well and refrigerate for 1 hour or overnight, until ready to make the crusts.
3. Generously flour a work surface. Divide the dough into thirds and roll out one piece at a time. Sprinkle with flour to avoid sticking. Roll each piece of dough as thin as possible (no more than ⅛ inch thick). Use an empty, clean, large-sized tuna can (or other 4-inch ring) to cut out rounds of dough. Stack the rounds in layers separated by wax paper until ready to make pies. You should have about 40 circles. The rounds can be covered and chilled for up to 1 day, or frozen, well wrapped, for up to 1 month. Let soften slightly before filling.

Chicken-Sage Filling

 4 tablespoons olive oil
 ¾ pound ground chicken
 3 garlic cloves, minced or passed through a garlic press

1 tablespoon chopped fresh sage
1½ teaspoons salt
1 teaspoon black pepper
¾ teaspoon fennel seeds
⅛ teaspoon crushed red pepper flakes
3 tablespoons all-purpose flour
½ medium onion, finely chopped
1 small green bell pepper, finely chopped
2 small celery stalks, finely chopped
1 small carrot, grated
1 teaspoon fresh thyme
Pinch of cayenne pepper
¾ cup chicken broth, canned or homemade (page 72)
1 large egg
1 tablespoon milk

1. Warm 1 tablespoon of the olive oil in a skillet over medium-high heat. Add the chicken, garlic, sage, ¾ teaspoon of the salt, ½ teaspoon of the black pepper, the fennel seeds, and red pepper flakes and sauté, breaking up the meat as you stir, until the chicken is cooked through, 5 to 7 minutes. Transfer the mixture to a large bowl.

2. Wipe out the skillet and add the remaining 3 tablespoons olive oil. Place over medium-high heat and let warm for 1 minute. Stir in the flour 1 tablespoon at a time. Continue to stir for 5 minutes more, or until the flour is dark amber-brown. Add the chopped and grated vegetables (this will stop the browning process), thyme, cayenne, and remaining ¾ teaspoon salt and ½ teaspoon pepper. Cook, stirring, until the vegetables are softened, about 5 minutes. Stir in the broth and bring to a bubble. Simmer until the roux has a thick, gravy-like consistency (more pasty than soupy), 3 to 5 minutes. Let cool slightly. Stir in the ground chicken mixture, cover, and refrigerate until chilled, about 30 minutes or up to 1 day. In a food processor or by hand, finely mince the chilled chicken mixture.

3. To form the pies, spoon 1 tablespoon of filling into the center of each pastry round. In a small bowl, whisk together the egg and milk and brush a bit of the wash onto the edge of each round before folding it over the filling to form a half circle (reserve the egg wash for baking). Crimp the edges with a fork to seal. The pies can be refrigerated between layers of wax paper (and make sure to cover the top layer of pies) for up to 8 hours before baking.

To Bake

    Olive oil, for brushing the pan

1. Preheat the oven to 450 degrees F and brush a cookie sheet with olive oil.
2. Place the pies on the cookie sheet and bake for 10 minutes. Remove from the oven and brush the tops of the pies with additional egg wash. Return the pies to the oven and bake until brown, about 10 minutes more. Serve warm.

CHAPTER 2

Salads

Sit-Down Sizzlin' Salad

One of the Ford family favorites was, and still is, wilted lettuce. Mom cornered the market with this dish. She had a particular way of preparing the red leaf lettuce and chopping the scallions. Everything had to be just right.

The most crucial step in the preparation was the final one: drizzling on the hot bacon drippings. The deal was, everything else had to be done first. I mean everything! The table had to be set, the rest of the meal put on the table, drinks poured, everything. But most important, we had to be seated.

Mom would say, "Charles!" (Charles is my dad.) "Charles, sit down! I'm about to wilt the lettuce!" My sister and I would sit. My dad would sit. We all knew not to fight this process because when it came time to drizzle the hot oil over that big bowl of tasty greens you had to be giving it your undivided attention.

When Mom said, "Okay, ready?" suddenly there it was, that sound: SSSS-sss, the sizzle of all those textures, tastes, and colors blending together at just the right moment, the reason for everything. Then she would spoon the salad onto our plates, carefully distributing every morsel of lettuce, scallions, and bacon. I salivate just thinking about my first sizzlin' bite of salad.

Sit-Down Sizzlin' Salad
(a.k.a. "Wilted Lettuce")

To cut the lettuce into strips, pile and roll several leaves into a tube, then slice them cross-wise. Wilt the lettuce at the last minute and then serve it all up because this salad is only good warm and has to be eaten immediately.

SERVES 4

> 1 large or 2 small heads red leaf lettuce,
>   cut into ½-inch strips (about 8 cups)
> 3 scallions, chopped into ¼-inch pieces
> 2 to 3 teaspoons white vinegar, to taste
> Salt
> 4 slices bacon

1. Place four salad bowls in a 200 degree F oven to warm them. Place the lettuce and scallions in a large metal, wood, thick glass, or ceramic salad bowl (don't use plastic). Sprinkle with the vinegar and a pinch of salt and toss well. Set aside.
2. In a heavy skillet over medium heat, fry the bacon until crisp, about 5 minutes. Transfer it to a paper towel–lined plate, leaving the drippings in the hot pan.
3. When everything else is on the table and everyone is ready to eat, reheat the drippings if necessary. Pour the hot bacon drippings over the lettuce a little at a time, tossing after each addition. Serve immediately in the warmed salad bowls with the bacon crumbled on top.

Faith's Sizzlin' Salad

My sizzlin' salad, with turkey bacon and balsamic, is a little different from my mother's, but no less delicious. If you want to make a vegetarian version, omit the bacon altogether, use very hot olive oil to wilt the lettuce, and garnish with vegetarian bacon bits if desired.

SERVES 4

> 1 large or 2 small bunches red leaf lettuce,
>   cut into ½-inch strips (about 8 cups)
> 3 scallions, white and light green parts only,
>   cut into ¼-inch pieces
> 2 to 3 teaspoons balsamic vinegar, to taste
> Salt
> ⅓ cup olive oil
> 4 slices turkey bacon

1. Place four salad bowls in a 200 degree F oven to warm them. Place the lettuce and scallions in a large metal, wood, thick glass, or ceramic salad bowl (don't use plastic). Sprinkle with the balsamic vinegar and a pinch of salt and toss well. Set aside.
2. In a heavy skillet over medium heat, warm the olive oil. Fry the turkey bacon in the olive oil until browned, about 8 minutes. Transfer it to a paper towel–lined plate, leaving the oil in the hot pan (if the turkey bacon has soaked up a lot of oil, add a little more to the pan).
3. When everything else is on the table and everyone is ready to eat, reheat the oil if necessary. Pour the hot oil over the lettuce a little at a time, tossing after each addition. Serve immediately in the warmed salad bowls with the turkey bacon crumbled on top.

Spinach Salad with Creamy Dill-Horseradish Dressing

I went through a brief vegetarian phase when I used to make a lot of spinach salads. I always ate them with a store-bought dressing that I loved, until one day it went off the market. It became an obsession of mine to recreate its creamy, tangy taste. Here's my version, which has horseradish and honey and is flecked with green dill. This salad is great served with fish, or you can turn it into a complete vegetarian meal by adding chickpeas, mushrooms, and beets.

SERVES 8

¼ cup nonfat plain yogurt
¼ cup light or regular mayonnaise
2 tablespoons olive oil
2 tablespoons cider vinegar
2 tablespoons finely chopped fresh dill
1 tablespoon bottled horseradish
1 teaspoon honey
1 shallot, minced
1 garlic clove, chopped
¼ teaspoon salt
¼ teaspoon black pepper
1 pound tender spinach leaves (about 10 cups)

1. Put the yogurt, mayonnaise, olive oil, vinegar, 1 tablespoon of the dill, the horseradish, honey, shallot, garlic, salt, and pepper in a blender or food processor and blend until smooth. Stir in the remaining tablespoon of dill by hand. Store covered in the refrigerator for up to 5 days.
2. When ready to serve, place the spinach in a large bowl, drizzle it with dressing to taste, and toss well. Serve immediately.

Arugula Salad with Honey-Mustard Dressing and Cheese Grits Croutons

So much of what I like to eat comes from memories of the foods I grew up with. For instance, arugula has a bitterness that reminds me of mustard greens. It grows really well in my L.A. garden, and paired with this tangy-sweet dressing, it has become my favorite salad.

Topped with crispy cheese grits croutons, arugula salad becomes much more substantial. And grits are the original comfort food for me. When I was a little girl they were sometimes all my mother could get me to eat.

Discovering how I could use up leftover grits and not waste one bite of them became my goal when I grew up. These croutons are perfect for that. My inspiration came from some polenta croutons I fell in love with at an Italian restaurant. One day I realized why I was so crazy about them—they reminded me of grits!

This recipe makes a lot. Scale it back if you want to, or store the dressing, croutons, and washed arugula separately in the fridge to use for several meals for fewer people. The dressing and croutons will keep for up to 5 days.

SERVES 8

Honey-Mustard Dressing
>   3 tablespoons olive oil
>   2 tablespoons vegetable oil
>   2 tablespoons white wine vinegar
>   2 tablespoons cider vinegar
>   2 tablespoons honey
>   1 tablespoon soy sauce
>   2 garlic cloves, chopped
>   2 teaspoons Dijon mustard
>   ½ teaspoon hot sauce, or to taste
>   ¼ teaspoon salt
>   ¼ teaspoon black pepper
>   ¼ teaspoon sweet paprika

Combine all the ingredients in a blender or food processor and blend until smooth. (You'll have about ⅔ cup dressing.) Store in a covered container in the refrigerator for up to 5 days.

Cheese Grits

1½ cups milk
1 cup grits
1 cup grated Parmesan cheese
1 large egg, beaten
1 tablespoon chopped fresh parsley, or ½ teaspoon dried parsley
1 garlic clove, minced or passed through a garlic press
1 teaspoon Dijon mustard
1 teaspoon salt
½ teaspoon black pepper
1 to 1½ cups plain dried bread crumbs

1. In a saucepan, combine the milk with 1½ cups water and bring to a boil over medium heat. Gradually pour in the grits, stirring as you pour to prevent lumps from forming. Simmer, stirring, until thickened, 5 to 7 minutes. Stir in the cheese, egg, parsley, garlic, mustard, salt, and pepper. Mix well, then transfer to a 9-by-9-inch pan and spread the grits evenly in the pan. Press plastic wrap directly onto the surface of the grits and refrigerate for at least 1 hour and up to 5 days.
2. Turn the grits out onto a board and cut them into ½-inch cubes. Place the bread crumbs in a shallow bowl and roll the cubes in them to cover. (At this point, the cubes can be frozen, well wrapped, for up to 1 month. Defrost before proceeding.)

To Serve

Olive oil, for brushing or spraying
4 bunches arugula (about 16 cups)

Preheat the broiler. Lightly brush or spray a nonstick baking pan with olive oil and arrange the cheese grits cubes on it in a single layer. Lightly brush or spray the cubes with more oil. Broil, turning frequently, until browned on all sides, 5 to 8 minutes. Serve immediately on a bed of arugula, drizzled with the honey-mustard dressing.

Brenda's Make-Ahead
Seven-Layer Salad

I've always been a big salad person. My mother would say, "We have to make a big salad for Faith. She's got to have her vegetables." Let me tell you, when I was a teenager, I was really excited when salad bars became a big thing!

I think of this layered concoction as a party salad, since my aunt Brenda used to make something like it for family gatherings. It's nice to bring to potlucks because you can make it in advance, which you can't do with all salads.

Mom Says: On holidays, Brenda and I would bring dishes to add to the big meal at our parents' home, and this salad was much requested. It makes a lot, enough so there was always plenty to divide and take home for "supper"—what we Southerners would call a light evening meal usually consisting of leftovers from the big midday "dinner." We always used canned peas in this recipe, but these days some people prefer frozen. For the authentic effect, substitute one 15-ounce can tiny green peas, drained, rinsed, and patted dry.

SERVES 12

2 hearts of romaine lettuce, chopped (6 to 8 cups)
1½ cups frozen tiny green peas, thawed and patted dry (see Mom Says)
1 green bell pepper, seeded and finely chopped
1 small red onion, finely chopped
2 cups light or regular mayonnaise
1 tablespoon sugar
2 ounces cheddar cheese, grated (about ½ cup)
8 slices pork or turkey bacon

1. In a deep salad bowl, layer the lettuce, peas, bell pepper, and onion. Use a rubber spatula to gently spread the mayonnaise over the top of the salad, all the way to the edges, so that the top is sealed. Sprinkle the sugar evenly over the mayonnaise, then sprinkle on the cheddar cheese. Place a piece of plastic wrap directly on top of the mayonnaise and refrigerate for at least 12 hours and up to 2 days.

2. To prepare the bacon, line a plate with paper towels. Place a skillet over medium-high heat and add the bacon. Fry until crisp, about 8 minutes. Transfer to the towel-lined plate and let cool, then crumble. The bacon can be made up to 4 hours in advance and stored uncovered at room temperature.

3. Just before serving, carefully remove the plastic wrap from the salad and sprinkle the bacon bits over the salad. To serve, scoop down to get some of each layer in each serving.

Even before I moved to Los Angeles, salads and greens were always a huge part of every supper.

Grandpa Walker's Favorite Crunchy Southern Slaw

My mom's dad loved coleslaw. But my grandma Cora wouldn't make it for him because she didn't like to eat anything raw. She wouldn't even eat fruit unless it was cooked in a pie or cobbler. "Oh," she'd say when confronted with a salad, "that is *not cooked.*"

And so my poor grandpa only got to eat coleslaw a few times a year. One occasion was when he got my mom to make it for him on New Year's Day. New Year's was his favorite meal; we'd have fresh pork roast with onion gravy, black-eyed peas for good luck and prosperity, and plenty of coleslaw. My mom's recipe was simple: basically, cabbage, salt, pepper, white vinegar, a little mayo, and some dill pickle for extra crunch.

Other than on New Year's, Grandpa could have coleslaw when he and my grandma drove up to Ferriday, Louisiana, to see his mother, Ma Walker, in a nursing home. They never ate any other fast food, but Grandma would tolerate the fried chicken chain in Ferriday, so Grandpa would get a treat of coleslaw and mashed potatoes.

SERVES 8

> 1 small green cabbage, shredded (about 6 cups)
> 1 medium carrot, grated
> ½ cup light or regular mayonnaise
> ¼ cup sweet pickle relish
> 1 tablespoon cider vinegar
> 1 teaspoon sugar
> 1 teaspoon black pepper
> ¾ teaspoon salt

Combine all the ingredients in a large bowl and toss to evenly coat the cabbage and carrot. Chill for at least 2 hours before serving. The slaw can be made 1 day ahead, covered with plastic wrap, and refrigerated.

Pleasingly Purple Cabbage Salad
with Basil Balsamic Dressing

I like to serve colorful vegetable side dishes that can be made ahead yet still keep their crunch. This pretty purple cabbage salad fits the bill perfectly, and the flavors definitely get better overnight. But if you don't have enough time, you can also make it a few hours ahead and leave it out at room temperature (a good thing if you are low on fridge space . . . I know I always am before entertaining). Since there's no mayo in it, it won't spoil, and it's great with burgers for a cookout.

Mom Says: Faith calls this a salad. I call it a slaw. You decide.

SERVES 12

¼ cup balsamic vinegar
¼ cup olive oil
¼ cup chopped fresh basil
2 garlic cloves
1 teaspoon salt
¼ teaspoon black pepper
½ large head purple cabbage, cored and shredded (6 cups)
1 medium carrot, grated
1 small red onion, chopped

1. Put the vinegar, olive oil, basil, garlic, salt, and pepper in a blender or food processor and blend until smooth. Cover and refrigerate for up to 3 days.
2. Mix the cabbage, carrot, and onion together in a large bowl. Add ½ cup of the dressing and toss well. Taste and add more dressing, salt, and pepper if necessary. Cover and leave out at room temperature for up to 3 hours, or refrigerate overnight.

Asian Cajun Slaw

Made with fresh ginger and peanuts, this is not your average Southern-style slaw. But just like Cajun food, many Asian dishes tend to be a little bit spicy and a little bit tangy, so these flavors are actually great together.

If you don't have peanuts in your cupboard but you do have peanut butter, just add a tablespoon or two to the dressing as an alternative to the chopped nuts. You'll end up with a creamier slaw. This goes great with po' boys, roast turkey, or even meat loaf

SERVES 4

2 tablespoons soy sauce
2 tablespoons rice vinegar
2 tablespoons honey
2 tablespoons Asian sesame oil or toasted sesame oil
½ to 1 teaspoon hot sauce, to taste
½ teaspoon finely chopped or grated fresh ginger
1 small cabbage, cored and shredded (about 6 cups)
½ small red onion, chopped
2 scallions, chopped
2 tablespoons chopped roasted unsalted peanuts (see page 244)

1. Put the soy sauce, vinegar, honey, sesame oil, hot sauce, and ginger in a blender or food processor and blend until smooth. Refrigerate in a covered container for up to 5 days.
2. In a large salad bowl, toss together the cabbage, onion, and scallions. Drizzle with dressing to taste and toss well. If desired, cover with plastic wrap and refrigerate for up to 1 day. Garnish with the peanuts just before serving.

Cora's Creamy Country Potato Salad

My grandma Cora used to love to make this homey salad. Starchy potatoes are mashed up like they would be for mashed potatoes, then mixed with onion, mayo, pickles, and hard-boiled eggs. The potatoes end up nice and fluffy, and since they're mixed with the other ingredients while still warm, they soak up a lot of good flavors. This salad was always on the table in the summertime when we had fried catfish (page 82). That wasn't the only time we ate it, but you didn't have catfish without it. My grandma would lure me over to the table, saying, "I've got some of that potato salad over here, Faithie." And I'd run right over.

SERVES 8

3 large baking potatoes (about 2 pounds), peeled and cut into 2-inch chunks
1 teaspoon salt
1 cup light or regular mayonnaise
3 large eggs, hard-boiled (see page 9) and chopped
½ small sweet white onion, chopped
¼ cup chopped bread and butter pickles (see page 256, for homemade)
½ teaspoon black pepper

1. In a medium saucepan, cover the potatoes with water and add ½ teaspoon of the salt. Bring to a boil, then reduce the heat to medium-high and cook for 10 to 12 minutes, until tender. Drain and cool to room temperature.
2. Mash the potatoes until creamy but not totally smooth—there should be some lumps. Add the mayonnaise, chopped egg, onion, pickles, remaining ½ teaspoon of salt, and the pepper and stir together. This can be made up to 1 day ahead and kept covered in the refrigerator. Serve at room temperature.

Faith's Old-Is-New Potato Salad

Recently, I started adding pimentos and pickle relish to my basic potato salad, and I thought of this as my invention. But then when I started writing the recipes for this book, my mom told me that Grandma Bernice would add pimentos and relish to hers, and, frankly, that the pimento and relish were what had been missing from mine all along! So maybe this recipe is not so new. But I do use new red potatoes and yogurt, which my grandma certainly never did. So this is my new, yet old, new potato salad!

SERVES 8

3½ pounds small red potatoes, cut into quarters
2 teaspoons salt
2 celery stalks, finely chopped
½ cup light or regular mayonnaise
½ cup nonfat plain yogurt
¼ small red onion, finely chopped
2 scallions, chopped
¼ cup sweet pickle relish
1 (4-ounce) jar pimentos, drained and chopped
2 tablespoons chopped fresh parsley, basil, or dill
   (use dill if you are serving this with seafood)
1 tablespoon Dijon mustard
1 tablespoon prepared horseradish
½ teaspoon black pepper
½ teaspoon hot chili powder

1. Place the potatoes in a large saucepan with water to cover and 1 teaspoon of the salt. Cover and bring to a boil. Adjust the lid so that it is slightly ajar and let the potatoes boil for 15 minutes, until tender. Drain and let cool to room temperature.
2. Meanwhile, in a small bowl, combine the celery, mayonnaise, yogurt, onion, scallions, pickle, pimentos, fresh herbs, mustard, horseradish, the remaining teaspoon of salt, the black pepper, and chili powder and mix together. Pour the mixture over the cooled potatoes and toss until evenly coated. This can be made up to 1 day ahead and kept covered in the refrigerator. Serve cool or at room temperature.

Cajun Grilled Vegetable Salad

These grilled vegetables are a staple in my house. I grill them outside in the summer and roast them in the oven the rest of the year. I serve them as they are, as a side dish, in sandwiches (see page 18) and soups, or this salad. Vary the veggies depending on what's in season or what you're in the mood for. Toss in some chopped tomato and avocado if desired.

SERVES 8

6 large portobello mushroom caps
2 yellow squash, cut lengthwise into ½-inch-thick slices
2 zucchini, cut lengthwise into ½-inch-thick slices
3 red bell peppers, quartered lengthwise, seeded, and cored
1 eggplant, cut lengthwise into ½-inch-thick slices
½ cup olive oil
1 tablespoon Faith's Special Seasoning (page 266) or
    Cajun seasoning (see Sources, page 267)
1 medium red onion, chopped
1 bunch fresh basil, chopped (about 1 cup)
¼ cup balsamic vinegar
1 teaspoon salt

1. Light the grill, preheat a stovetop grill, or preheat the oven to 425 degrees F.
2. Place all the sliced vegetables in a large bowl. Add the olive oil and Faith's seasoning and toss well.
3. Grill the vegetables, using a grilling basket if desired, turning them every 5 minutes and moving them around the grill, taking care that they don't burn, until sear marks appear and they are cooked through, 10 to 15 minutes. Alternatively, spread the vegetables in a single layer on a baking sheet and roast until golden and tender, 20 to 25 minutes, turning once or twice to ensure even cooking.
4. Chop the grilled vegetables into bite-sized chunks. They can be served warm, or made up to 3 hours ahead of time and kept at room temperature, covered with foil. Just before serving, place the vegetables in a large bowl and add the onion, basil, vinegar, and salt and toss to combine. Serve warm or at room temperature.

Bernice's English Pea Salad

My grandma Bernice offered this cold salad every time we went to her house. She would use her homemade pickles in it and serve it in a cute blue bowl. It was an especially nice salad to have in the summertime with our fish fries. And it's very easy to make ahead of time.

SERVES 4 TO 6

3 large eggs, hard-boiled (see page 9) and chopped

1½ cups frozen tiny green peas, thawed and drained (or canned, see Mom Says, page 36)

⅓ cup light or regular mayonnaise

½ small red onion, finely chopped

½ cup chopped dill pickles

½ green bell pepper, chopped

1 (4-ounce) jar pimentos, drained and chopped

Sweet paprika

1. In a large salad bowl, combine the chopped eggs, peas, mayonnaise, onion, pickles, bell pepper, and pimentos and toss gently to combine.
2. Cover and chill for at least 2 hours and up to 1 day. Sprinkle with paprika just before serving.

Faith's Fresh Petite Pea Salad

My pea salad is spicier and zestier than the one my grandma Bernice made (opposite). I use her basic recipe as a guide, then brighten it up with fresh peas instead of canned or frozen, and fresh basil, tomato, pepperoncini, and Creole mustard. It goes great with fried chicken (see pages 94 to 98) or Southern-Style Fried Catfish (see page 82).

SERVES 8

2 cups shelled petite green peas (from about 2 pounds unshelled)

2 large eggs, hard-boiled (see page 9), whites chopped (reserve the yolks for another purpose)

1 celery stalk, chopped

½ small red onion, chopped

½ cup chopped kalamata or niçoise olives

½ cup light or regular mayonnaise

½ medium tomato, seeded and chopped

¼ cup thinly sliced fresh basil leaves

¼ cup chopped sweet pickle

¼ cup chopped pickled pepperoncini pepper

1 teaspoon Creole mustard (see Sources, page 267) or spicy brown mustard (see Note, page 23)

½ teaspoon black pepper

1. Bring a small pot of salted water to a boil and add the peas. Blanch the peas until just tender, about 3 minutes, then drain them in a colander and rinse under cold water to stop the cooking. Drain well.

2. In a bowl, combine the remaining ingredients. Fold in the peas, cover with plastic wrap, and chill for at least 2 hours before serving. The salad can be made up to 1 day in advance.

Warm Black-Eyed Pea Salad

I developed this salad when I worked on *Murphy Brown*. That's when I started entertaining a lot in my first little house in L.A., and really started to understand what folks in this city do and do not like to eat. Since everyone knew I was from the South, they wanted me to make Southern dishes. But they didn't want fried foods or all the fat that goes into a lot of Southern cooking. They wanted lighter and healthier foods with the same flavors. So I came up with this black-eyed pea salad, which everyone loves, especially me. One huge benefit is that there's no meat in it, so it's good for vegetarians, and in L.A. there are usually a few at every party. You can make it in advance and it keeps well, even at room temperature, for several hours, so it doesn't need any last-minute fussing. It goes with a lot of things, including chicken, grilled fish, and pork.

SERVES 8

> 4 tablespoons olive oil
> 6 garlic cloves, chopped
> 2 (15-ounce) cans black-eyed peas, rinsed and drained, or
>   2 (10-ounce) packages frozen black-eyed peas, thawed
> 1 teaspoon salt
> 2 large tomatoes, seeded and chopped
> 2 celery stalks, finely chopped
> ⅓ cup chopped fresh basil
> ½ small red onion, finely chopped
> 1 tablespoon balsamic vinegar

1. In a 1- or 2-quart saucepan, warm 2 tablespoons of the olive oil over medium heat. Add 4 cloves of the garlic and sauté until lightly browned, about 1 minute. Add the black-eyed peas, 1 cup water, and the salt. Cover and simmer for 5 to 20 minutes (canned take less time than frozen) until the peas are flavorful and tender.
2. In a large bowl, combine the tomatoes, celery, basil, onion, remaining 2 tablespoons olive oil, remaining 2 cloves garlic, and the balsamic vinegar. Toss well.
3. Strain the peas and add them to the bowl. Toss well to thoroughly coat them with dressing. This salad can be made up to 2 days ahead, covered with plastic wrap, and refrigerated. Serve warm or at room temperature.

Warm Corn Salad with Bacon and Sage

I love the combination of sweet and salty. This recipe evolved from my grandma Cora's creamed skillet corn, which was made with bacon, so it had a smoky-sweet flavor. Since I can't have the yellow corn shucked fresh from my grandma Cora's garden, I use the freshest white corn I can find and grill it with a tiny bit of maple syrup, which gives the closest taste, or else I substitute frozen white corn. My grandma would have been proud to see this book, but I bet she'd say, "This corn needs to be cooked a little more!" She never liked vegetables to be crunchy.

SERVES 6

> 6 slices bacon or turkey bacon
> 1 to 2 tablespoons olive oil
> 1 medium red onion, chopped
> 1 garlic clove, minced or passed through a garlic press
> 2 (10-ounce) packages frozen sweet white or
>   yellow corn kernels (4 cups)
> ¼ cup chopped fresh sage
> 1 teaspoon chopped pickled jalapeño, or 2 tablespoons
>   chopped fresh jalapeño, optional
> 1 teaspoon Faith's Special Seasoning (see page 266) or
>   Cajun seasoning (see Sources, page 267)
> ½ teaspoon salt

1. In a heavy skillet over medium heat, cook the bacon until crisp, about 5 minutes (cook the turkey bacon in 1 tablespoon olive oil). Transfer to a paper towel–lined plate to drain. When the slices have cooled, break them into small pieces.
2. If you used regular bacon, drain all but 1 tablespoon of the bacon grease from the pan. Add the olive oil. Add the onion and garlic and sauté until golden brown and transparent, 5 to 7 minutes. Add the corn and sauté for 5 minutes more.
3. Remove the pan from the heat and toss in the bacon, sage, jalapeño, Faith's seasoning, and salt. Serve immediately or at room temperature. The salad can be made up to 6 hours ahead, but don't refrigerate it, just keep it covered.

Warm Pasta Salad with Chicken Andouille Sausage, Mustard Greens, and Black-Eyed Peas

All the flavors in this dish are Southern, but it's definitely not something my grandma would have ever made. She only discovered pasta (such as spaghetti) when she was in her seventies. And often, when people in the South made spaghetti, they would do it as a casserole in the crockpot, with meat sauce. It tastes good but would horrify anyone who subscribes to the Italian view of firm-cooked (al dente) pasta.

When I make pasta, it has to be al dente, preferably with a lot of fresh and healthful ingredients like the chicken sausage and greens in this recipe. This is a great family meal—it takes only about thirty minutes to make, feeds a lot of people, and it's filling. I love it when Campion has some of his guy friends around, watching a game, because I can test out my recipes on them. This one was a winner from the get-go.

> ### ANDOUILLE AND TASSO
>
> These spicy Cajun meats are used in red beans and gumbos, or whenever a smoky flavor is needed. Andouille (pronounced ahn-DOO-wee) is a seasoned pork sausage (chicken andouille is made from chicken and is leaner) that is smoked until almost hard. Tasso is made from lean pork butt (turkey tasso is made from lean turkey thigh) that has been heavily seasoned with pepper, vinegar, mustard, and garlic, then smoked. Both are available by mail order (see Sources, page 267).

⇥ *Mom Says:* Don't throw out those leftovers! Two cups of Red-Hot Black-Eyed Peas (page 158) can be substituted for the black-eyed peas and diced tomato here.

4 tablespoons olive oil

1 tablespoon salt

12 ounces chicken andouille or other spicy sausage, sliced

4 garlic cloves, thinly sliced

1½ large bunches mustard greens, chopped (about 8 cups)

1 cup canned spicy diced tomatoes (or substitute regular diced tomatoes and add hot sauce to taste)

1 cup frozen or canned black-eyed peas (see Sources, page 267)

1 tablespoon Creole mustard (see Note, page 23)

½ cup chicken broth, canned or homemade (page 72)

1 pound rotini pasta

1 tablespoon soy sauce

½ teaspoon hot sauce, or to taste

1. Fill a large pot with water and add 1 tablespoon of the olive oil and the salt. Bring to a boil.
2. Heat 2 tablespoons of the olive oil in a large skillet over medium-high heat. Add the sausage and cook until brown, about 5 minutes. Add the garlic and sauté until softened and fragrant, 1 to 2 minutes more. Add the mustard greens and cook, stirring, until the greens are wilted, 3 to 5 minutes. Stir in the tomatoes, black-eyed peas, mustard, chicken broth, and additional salt to taste. Lower the heat, cover, and simmer for 5 minutes.
3. Cook the pasta in the boiling water until al dente.
4. Whisk together the remaining tablespoon of olive oil, the soy sauce, and hot sauce in a large serving bowl. Drain the pasta, add it to the bowl, and toss until well coated. Transfer the pasta to the skillet with the sausage mixture. Sauté for 1 minute to blend all the flavors, then return to the serving bowl. Serve hot.

CHAPTER 3

Soups, Gumbos, and Chilis

Broccoli Ginger Soup

I became a big fan of fresh ginger when someone told me it was good for you (it has anti-viral properties that can help fight colds and flu). I was already living in L.A. at the time. When I was growing up, the only ginger I knew was the ground kind in gingersnaps, one of my mother's favorite store-bought cookies. Fresh ginger is not something you typically find in Louisiana. Now that I've discovered it I have started putting it in soups when I don't feel well. It's healthy, and it also tastes great.

Every now and then my husband and I go on a nonmeat diet for a while. One of the things we love is this soup. It's simple and quick, and tastes clean. Make it for yourself or serve it to a crowd instead of a whole bunch of appetizers. Since it's mostly vegetable, you don't need a salad with it.

SERVES 8

> 8 cups vegetable or chicken broth, canned or homemade (page 73 or 72)
> 1 large onion, chopped
> 2 tablespoons finely chopped fresh ginger
> 3 garlic cloves, chopped
> 3 large broccoli heads, stems peeled, stems and florets chopped
> ½ to 1 teaspoon salt, to taste
> ¼ teaspoon black pepper
> Freshly squeezed lemon juice, for serving, optional
> Chopped fresh parsley

1. Pour the broth into a stockpot and add the onion, ginger, and garlic. Bring to a boil, reduce the heat, and simmer for 20 minutes. Add the broccoli, salt, and pepper and simmer until the broccoli is very tender, about 15 minutes.
2. Use an immersion blender to puree the soup in the pot. Or transfer it, in small batches, to a stand blender and puree until smooth. This soup can be made ahead and refrigerated, covered, for up to 2 days. Reheat or serve chilled, and drizzle with lemon juice if desired. Garnish with parsley.

My Sister's Soothing Soup

My sister, Devon O'Day, is an amazing person. She lives on a farm where she keeps horses, ducks, chickens, cats, and dogs. She's the producer of a radio show, writes songs, and does voiceovers, and she's also the author of a collection of short stories about animal rescues called *My Angels Wear Fur*. Right now, she's working on a sequel.

Given how busy she is, it's not surprising that she likes to cook things that are fast and fairly simple. This is exactly the kind of soup she makes when she comes home from work and doesn't feel like eating a heavy evening meal. It's incredibly soothing, and my sister swears it has healing qualities. I don't argue with my big sis—she's usually right!

SERVES 8

2 tablespoons olive oil
1 medium onion, chopped
3 garlic cloves, chopped
½ head cabbage, shredded (about 4 cups)
1 teaspoon salt
4 cups chicken or vegetable broth, canned or homemade (pages 72 to 73)
2 large russet potatoes, peeled and cut into ½-inch chunks
1 (28-ounce) can diced tomatoes
¼ cup chopped fresh parsley
2 teaspoons hot sauce, or to taste, optional

1. In a stockpot over medium-high heat, warm the oil. Add the onion and garlic and sauté until tender, about 5 minutes. Add the cabbage and salt and sauté until wilted, about 3 minutes.
2. Add the broth, 2 cups water, the potatoes, and the tomatoes and bring to a boil. Reduce the heat to medium and simmer, covered, for 20 to 30 minutes, until the potatoes are tender. Stir in the parsley, hot sauce, and additional salt to taste.

Cures What Ails Ya Chicken Soup

This is the soup to make if you or someone you love feels ill—or if you just want some chicken soup. It only takes 15 to 20 minutes to prepare. I pour the hot soup over a bowl of spinach, which wilts immediately. It's delicious and very healthful, and full of garlic, ginger, and lemon juice in addition to greens. I always try to keep these ingredients on hand during the cold season just in case. You never know when you might have to ward off some bug. Any leftover soup can be kept in the fridge and then thinned with more broth if needed before serving again.

SERVES 6

2 tablespoons olive oil
1 small onion, chopped
2 to 4 garlic cloves, to taste, chopped
1 tablespoon grated or chopped fresh ginger
1 large carrot, chopped
1 celery stalk, chopped
1 tablespoon fresh thyme
8 cups chicken broth, canned or homemade (page 72)
1 whole roasted chicken (homemade or from the deli section of
    the grocery store—see Mom Says, page 102)
10 ounces fresh green beans, trimmed and snapped in half
1 tablespoon freshly squeezed lemon juice (from ½ lemon)
½ cup chopped fresh parsley
Salt and black pepper
6 ounces fresh baby spinach, coarsely chopped (about 6 cups)

1. Warm the olive oil in a medium stockpot over medium-high heat. Add the onion and sauté until it begins to soften, about 2 to 3 minutes. Add the garlic and ginger and sauté for a minute more. Add the carrot and celery and sauté for another minute. Add the thyme, stir, then add the broth and bring to a boil. Reduce the heat to low and simmer for 5 to 10 minutes, or until the vegetables are just tender.

2. While the soup is simmering, pull the chicken meat from the bones, remove and discard the skin, and cut the meat into bite-sized pieces. Stir into the soup. Add the green

beans and bring the heat to medium. The beans should be bright green and lightly cooked in 5 to 10 minutes. Stir in the lemon juice, parsley, and salt and pepper to taste. The soup can be made a day ahead, cooled, covered, and refrigerated. Reheat it before serving.

3. Put 1 cup of spinach into each of 6 bowls. Pour soup over the spinach and watch the spinach wilt. Serve immediately.

Grandma Bernice, my aunt Katherine, and me.

Spicy Chicken Soup with Fresh Green Chiles

This savory soup is perfect to serve when a crowd comes over to watch a football game (my husband, Campion, is really into sports) or the Oscars on TV. It's got a lot going on in it—almost like a chili—and it's fun for a group because there are garnishes for people to add themselves: fresh cilantro, avocado, cheese, and blue corn chips. I like to add plenty of hot sauce to my bowl, but I've learned that a lot of people out here in Los Angeles don't like things too spicy or too salty. The ones who do get invited over more often! Even Campion didn't like spicy food when I first met him, but I've trained his taste buds. Now he loves it. Spice is good for your metabolism and your sinuses, but you do need to balance it with something mellow: a little starch in the background, like rice, bread, or in this case, corn chips.

SERVES 12 TO 16 AS AN APPETIZER, 8 AS A MAIN COURSE

Chicken

> 3 skinless bone-in whole chicken breasts (about 3 pounds)
> ¼ cup mild chili powder
> 1 tablespoon salt
> ¼ cup freshly squeezed lime juice (from 2 limes)
> 3 tablespoons olive oil

1. Wash and pat the chicken breasts dry. Mix together the chili powder and salt and rub into each chicken breast. Place the breasts in a large resealable plastic bag or a bowl with a lid.
2. In a small bowl, whisk together the lime juice and olive oil and pour the mixture over the breasts. Seal the bag or cover the bowl and rotate to coat the chicken well. Let marinate for an hour at room temperature or overnight in the refrigerator.

Soup

3 tablespoons olive oil

1 large onion, chopped

2 celery stalks, chopped

3 garlic cloves, chopped

8 cups chicken broth, canned or homemade (page 72)

2 (14-ounce) cans diced tomatoes

2 cups frozen or fresh sweet white or yellow corn (from 4 ears
   if using fresh corn)

5 poblano chiles (or other mild whole green chile), roasted,
   peeled, and coarsely chopped (see Roasting Peppers, page 21)

1 tablespoon hot sauce, or to taste

1 teaspoon ground cumin

1 to 3 teaspoons salt, to taste

1 (14-ounce) can black beans, rinsed and drained

2 tablespoons freshly squeezed lime juice (from 1 lime)

1 large bag (about 12 ounces) blue or regular corn chips

2 avocados, cubed

2 cups shredded cheddar cheese

½ cup chopped fresh cilantro

1. In a large stockpot over medium-high heat, warm the olive oil. Sear the chicken breasts one or two at a time until well browned, about 7 minutes on each side. Transfer to a bowl and set aside.

2. Add the onion, celery, and garlic to the pot and sauté on medium heat for 1 to 2 minutes. Add the broth and 6 cups water; cover and bring to a boil. Put the sautéed chicken back in the pot and simmer over medium heat for 30 to 40 minutes, or until the chicken is tender. Remove the chicken and set aside until it is cool enough to handle.

3. Add the tomatoes, corn, chiles, hot sauce, cumin, and salt to the pot. Bring to a rolling boil, lower the heat, and simmer for 10 to 15 minutes more.

4. While the soup is simmering, remove the chicken from the bones and cut the meat into 2-inch pieces, then return them to the soup. Stir in the black beans and lime juice and simmer for 2 more minutes. The soup can be made 3 days ahead, cooled, covered, and refrigerated. Reheat before serving.

5. Ladle hot soup over the corn chips and top with avocado, cheese, and cilantro.

Roasted Vegetable Soup with Turkey Meatballs

I got the idea to make turkey meatballs from my friend, the actress Valerie Bertinelli. In her family, there's a tradition of making turkey meatball soup after Thanksgiving, using the leftover turkey carcass for the broth and fresh ground turkey for the meatballs. I thought the meatballs were so terrific that I started making them year-round. They're a great way to add protein to my roasted-vegetable soup, a staple in my house because I love roasting and grilling vegetables and always end up making too much. I transform the leftovers into soup, which is completely vegetarian until you add the meatballs. I usually cook them separately and serve them on the side when I'm entertaining because you never know if one of your guests may be vegetarian. Although I love the heartiness and protein the meatballs contribute, the soup, made from five different vegetables roasted with herbs and spices, is also delicious without them.

The vegetable stock and vegetable seasoning can be made well in advance, while the meatballs can be made up to a day ahead. If you want to serve a heartier main-course soup, double the meatball recipe. Also, turkey meatballs can be added to your favorite pasta sauce or other soups. Once you start making them you'll want to put them in everything!

SERVES 8

Turkey Meatballs

    3 tablespoons olive oil
    1 medium onion, finely chopped
    1 pound ground white turkey meat
    1 pound ground dark turkey meat
    2 garlic cloves, chopped
    2 teaspoons Faith's Special Seasoning (page 266) or
       Cajun seasoning (see Sources, page 267)
    1 teaspoon dried oregano
    1 teaspoon crushed red pepper flakes

1. In a cast-iron or other heavy skillet over medium heat, warm 1 tablespoon of the oil. Add the onion and cook, stirring, until well browned, about 7 minutes. Let cool.

2. In a bowl, combine the browned onion with the turkey, garlic, Faith's seasoning, oregano, and red pepper flakes.

3. Line several baking sheets or platters with wax paper. Form the turkey mixture into 1-inch balls and lay them out on the wax paper. At this point, you can either proceed with the soup or cover the meatballs with plastic wrap and refrigerate for up to 1 day or freeze for up to 1 month. Defrost before proceeding.

4. In a large cast-iron pan over medium-high heat, warm the remaining 2 tablespoons of oil. Add half the meatballs and cook, turning frequently, until browned on all sides, about 5 minutes. Cover the pan, reduce the heat to low, and cook for another 5 to 10 minutes, until the centers are no longer pink. Transfer the meatballs to a paper towel–lined plate and repeat the process with the remaining meatballs. Cooked meatballs can be made a day ahead, cooled, covered, refrigerated, and reheated in the soup.

Roasted Vegetables

Olive oil, for brushing (or spraying) on vegetables
3 Japanese eggplants, halved lengthwise
3 ears fresh sweet corn, shucked
3 medium zucchini, halved lengthwise
3 medium yellow squash, halved lengthwise
2 red bell peppers, quartered lengthwise, seeded and cored
4 teaspoons Faith's Special Seasoning (page 266) or
    Cajun seasoning (see Sources, page 267)
8 cups chicken or vegetable broth, canned or homemade (pages 72 to 73)
Chopped fresh parsley
Grated Parmesan cheese

1. Preheat the oven to 400 degrees F.

2. Lightly brush or spray four rimmed baking sheets with olive oil and divide the eggplant, corn, zucchini, squash, and bell peppers evenly among them (or use two baking sheets and roast the vegetables in batches). Sprinkle 1 teaspoon of Faith's seasoning over each pan. Brush or spray a little more oil over the vegetables and roast for 20 minutes.

3. Switch the position of the pans from top to bottom and back to front to ensure that they roast evenly and roast for another 20 minutes. Take out any vegetables that have begun to soften and brown, turn the rest over, and brush or spray the eggplant and corn with a little more oil if they seem very dry. Continue to roast until the vegetables

are soft (the corn will stay a little crunchy, but this adds texture to the soup), up to 20 minutes more. Let the vegetables cool slightly.

4. When the vegetables are cool enough to handle, cut the kernels off the corn by holding each ear in a wide bowl and sliding a sharp knife along the cob. Cut the other vegetables into ½- to 1-inch cubes.

5. Bring the broth to a simmer in a stockpot, add the roasted vegetables, cover, and heat gently. Add the meatballs to the soup and bring to a boil, then reduce the heat and simmer, uncovered, for 5 minutes or until they are heated through. Serve bowls of the soup garnished with parsley and Parmesan.

COOKING WITH FAITH

Black-Eyed Pea Soup with Sausage and Mustard Greens

Here's another hearty soup that takes well to variation. I like this with a mix of turkey and pork sausage, but you can use either all turkey or all pork sausage. Or, if you have any left-over meat from a pork roast or roasted turkey, add that instead (add any cooked meat at the end, though, just to heat it through). The mustard greens make this colorful and give a nice, fresh tang. And, of course, they're really good for you.

SERVES 8

> 2 tablespoons olive oil
> 1 pound turkey sausage (kielbasa or andouille), sliced
> ½ pound pork sausage, casings removed
> 1 large onion, chopped
> 3 celery stalks, chopped
> 10 cups chicken broth, canned or homemade (page 72)
> 3 (16-ounce) packages frozen black-eyed peas, or 3 (14-ounce) cans, drained
> 1 large bunch mustard greens, coarsely chopped (about 6 cups)
> Salt and black pepper

1. Warm the olive oil in a large, heavy stockpot over medium heat. Add the turkey and pork sausages and sauté until brown around the edges, about 5 minutes. Add the onion and celery and sauté for 5 minutes more. Add the chicken broth and bring to a boil, skimming off any excess foam that comes to the top.

2. Add the black-eyed peas and simmer for 15 minutes. Add the mustard greens and simmer until tender, about 15 minutes more.

3. Add salt and pepper to taste, cover, turn off the heat, and let sit for an hour or so. The flavors will meld as it sits. The soup can be made 3 days in advance, cooled, covered, and stored in the refrigerator. Reheat before serving.

Spicy Turkey Chili

Sure, chili is a terrific thing to serve to a crowd, but this recipe is so easy I like to make it on weeknights for just Campion and me (leftovers freeze well for up to 2 months). If you don't feel like making a salad to go along with this, you can serve the chili on top of plenty of shredded lettuce, which also helps tone down the heat if one of your guests thinks it's too spicy (never a problem in our house). Chili is also great with corn chips, but cornbread is more traditionally Southern. Or you can serve it with rice.

SERVES 8

> 2 teaspoons olive oil
> 1 large onion, chopped
> 2 pounds ground turkey
> 2 garlic cloves, chopped
> 4 to 5 tablespoons mild chili powder, to taste
> 3 tablespoons all-purpose flour
> 2 tablespoons salt, or to taste
> 1 (12-ounce) can or 2 (6-ounce) cans tomato paste
> Shredded cheddar cheese
> Chopped scallions
> Hot sauce

1. Warm the olive oil in a stockpot with a heavy bottom. Add the onion and sauté over high heat until browned, about 10 minutes. Add the turkey and continue cooking until the meat loses its red color, about 7 minutes. Reduce the heat to medium-low. Add the garlic and cook for 2 more minutes.
2. Stir in the chili powder, flour, and salt. Cook for 1 minute, stirring, and then add the tomato paste and cook for 3 minutes longer. Gradually stir in 5 cups water.
3. Raise the heat to bring the mixture to a boil, stirring constantly. Then reduce the heat to a slight simmer. Cook, covered, for 30 minutes to an hour, until thickened as much as you like it. Stir the pot often, reaching all the way to the bottom. Add more salt if desired and let sit, covered, until serving time, but no longer than 1 hour. Otherwise,

you can cool the chili, cover it, and refrigerate for up to 3 days, then heat it up before serving.

4. Serve the chili topped with shredded cheese and scallions; and provide a bottle of your favorite hot sauce so your guests can spice it up as much as they like.

There's never any extra space on the stove once I get going.
Here I am cooking for friends in my L.A. kitchen!

Mama's Vegetable Beef Soup

Since my grandpa Walker had cows, we didn't have to buy our meat when I was growing up. Instead, every half-year or so we would get our meat all wrapped up in little white packets and labeled for us, cut the way Grandpa wanted it and ready for the freezer. Now these were free-range cattle, no hormones or fattening up. The first time I had meat that wasn't from my grandpa's cattle (other than a fast food burger) was in New York, and I can remember thinking "this doesn't taste right." We'd eat at nice steak places, and I thought the meat tasted odd. The beef that we got from Grandpa's farm was sweet and wholesome, never tough or gristly. Even the stew meat and the soup bones were good. Whenever we wanted beef soup in the fall and winter, we'd just pull one of those little white packets from the freezer, along with some summer vegetables we'd put up. Hearty and filling, my mama's beef soup with cornbread is just home for me.

⇨ **Mom Says:** Always save the remainder of a beef roast and the leftover juice or gravy to use in beef soup. If you have already cooked the meat, you can skip sautéing it. Make the soup with all the vegetables, then add the cubed beef last so as not to overcook it. I always freeze some containers of soup for a nice quick lunch or light evening meal in the winter.

SERVES 8

1 tablespoon vegetable oil

1½ pounds lean beef stew meat, cut into 1½-inch cubes

2 teaspoons salt

1 large onion, chopped

1 garlic clove, minced, optional

5 cups water

2 (15-ounce) cans diced tomatoes

1 (15-ounce) can tomato sauce

1 large russet potato, peeled and cubed

8 medium pods fresh okra, trimmed and sliced ½ inch thick (about 2 cups), or
    1 (10-ounce) package frozen sliced okra

2 cups sweet white or yellow corn kernels, from 2 ears fresh corn, or
    1 (10-ounce) package frozen kernels

1 (10-ounce) package frozen butterbeans or baby lima beans
2 large carrots, sliced
2 celery stalks, sliced
Hot sauce, optional

1. In a stockpot over medium-high heat, warm the oil. Add the meat, sprinkle with 1 teaspoon of the salt, and sauté until the meat browns on all sides, 10 to 15 minutes. Add the onion and garlic and sauté for another 8 to 10 minutes. Add the water, raise the heat to high, and bring to a boil. Reduce the heat to medium-low and cover when there is just a slow bubble. Cook for 30 minutes, stirring occasionally.
2. Add the tomatoes, tomato sauce, potato, and vegetables to the meat. Add the remaining teaspoon of salt. Bring the mixture to a boil, then reduce the heat, cover, and let simmer for another 30 minutes, or until the meat and vegetables are done to your taste. The soup can be made 3 days in advance, cooled, covered, and stored in the refrigerator or frozen for up to 3 months. Reheat and serve with hot sauce on the side.

North Louisiana Smoked
Turkey Gumbo

Some gumbos have seafood in them, and sometimes you just use whatever you've got: chicken, andouille sausage, or in this case, smoked turkey. For an authentic gumbo, you start with a browned mixture of shortening and flour called a roux and then add your vegetables, some broth, and the seafood or meat. I always have gumbo when I'm in Louisiana. Outsiders will often put tomato in it, and sometimes it's too thick, like a bisque. We never use tomato, and we make ours thin and brothy. And you never have it in the South without gumbo filé on top. Every Louisiana home has a little bottle of this seasoning made of powdered sassafras leaves (see Sources, page 267); it's what really makes gumbo. It's close to powdered sage in flavor, very earthy and piney with a slight bitterness, and it thickens soups and stews. To be honest, it's an acquired taste. Campion's not crazy about it yet, but I sprinkle a little bit on his gumbo so he'll develop a taste for it. He's developed a taste for a lot of things he never thought he'd eat.

This particular gumbo is my aunt Brenda's recipe. She loves having smoked turkey for Thanksgiving—we'd bring a regular roasted turkey and she'd bring a smoked one—and she'd make smoked turkey gumbo with the leftovers. And it is amazing, with a great savory flavor.

⇨ *Mom Says:* There's no set way to make gumbo. Just as with any other soup, everyone makes it differently. But for an authentic gumbo, sprinkle ¼ teaspoon gumbo filé over everyone's bowls before serving. Filé is always added after cooking and just prior to serving. And do not skip the hot sauce—it's a must!

SERVES 4

> 5 cups chicken broth, canned or homemade (see page 72)
> 1 smoked turkey wing (see Sources, page 267)
> ½ cup vegetable oil
> ½ cup all-purpose flour
> 1 large onion, chopped
> Leafy tops of a bunch of celery, chopped (about ½ cup)
> 3 garlic cloves, chopped

½ pound andouille sausage or tasso, regular or turkey (see page 48)
2 smoked turkey legs, meat removed and cut into pieces
Salt and black pepper
Hot sauce
Cooked white rice
1 bunch scallions, chopped (about 1 cup)

1. In a medium saucepan with a lid, combine the chicken broth and turkey wing and bring to a boil. Reduce the heat and simmer, covered, for 1 hour. Remove the wing, let it cool, then pull off the meat and cut it into bite-sized pieces. Reserve the meat and broth separately.
2. Warm the oil in a cast-iron pot or Dutch oven over medium heat. Stir in the flour and cook, stirring constantly, until the roux is dark brown, about 10 minutes (careful not to let it burn!). Add the onion, celery tops, and garlic and cook until softened, 5 to 7 minutes.
3. Stir in the reserved chicken broth and bring to a boil. Add the andouille or tasso, reduce the heat to low, and simmer, uncovered, for 1 hour, stirring occasionally.
4. Add the chopped meat from the turkey legs and wing and season to taste with salt, pepper, and hot sauce. Raise the heat and bring the soup to a boil, then lower the heat to medium and cook at a lively simmer for 5 more minutes.
5. Serve over rice garnished with scallions. This can be made up to 3 days ahead and cooled, covered, refrigerated, or frozen for up to 2 months. Reheat before serving.

Shrimp Gumbo with Turkey Andouille

This is the kind of gumbo that non-Southerners imagine when they think of gumbo. It's a nice soupy stew of shrimp, sausage, and herbs flavored with the Cajun combo of onion, celery, and green bell peppers. Making a quick broth with the shrimp shells is easy and gives the gumbo a much richer taste.

🌿 *Mom Says:* This is the best gumbo I have ever had. It's not too thick, but just right. You can sprinkle a pinch of gumbo filé (see page 66) over the top of each bowl if you prefer.

SERVES 8

½ cup plus 2 tablespoons vegetable oil
1 pound smoked turkey andouille or sausage, sliced (see Sources, page 267)
1 small onion, chopped
3 garlic cloves, minced or passed through a garlic press
2 pounds medium shrimp, peeled and deveined, shells and tails reserved
½ cup all-purpose flour
3 celery stalks, chopped
1 green bell pepper, chopped
3 bay leaves
1 teaspoon dried thyme
1 teaspoon salt
½ teaspoon black pepper
¼ teaspoon cayenne pepper
Cooked white rice

1. In a heavy-bottomed pot over medium-high heat, warm the 2 tablespoons oil. Add the sausage and sauté until lightly browned, about 5 minutes. Transfer the sausage to a plate and drain the fat from the pot.
2. Add 8 cups water to the pot, ¼ cup of the chopped onion, the garlic, and the reserved

shells and tails from the shrimp. Bring to a boil and then let simmer for 20 minutes. Strain and reserve the broth, discarding the solids.

3. Wipe out the pot with paper towels. Over medium-high heat, warm the ½ cup oil. Add the flour and stir constantly until the roux is a rich brown but not burned, about 5 minutes. Stir in the remaining onion, the celery, and the bell pepper until coated with roux. Add 6 cups of the shrimp broth, the browned sausage, bay leaves, thyme, salt, black pepper, and cayenne and bring the mixture to a boil. Reduce the heat and simmer for 20 to 30 minutes.

4. If the liquid is too thick, add more broth and bring the gumbo back to a boil. Add the shrimp and cook for about 3 minutes, until the shrimp turn pink and curl. Remove from the heat and serve over rice. You can make this up to 3 days ahead, cool, cover, and refrigerate, then reheat it gently before serving.

Red Beans and Rice
with Andouille

I don't get to make this dish much now that I live in California because we never have red beans and rice weather here. In Louisiana, the time of year for red beans and rice is in the fall, when catfish season is done and the crawfish aren't ready yet. It's such a warm, cozy dish; when the leaves are just starting to change and you feel that breeze blowing in from the north, you get in the mood for red beans and rice. You can make it on a Sunday afternoon for an early dinner. It's great with cornbread, and it freezes well.

⚜ *Mom Says:* We like to cook red beans with a little baking soda to help make them easier to digest. Faith likes to serve this traditional dish with basmati rice instead of regular white rice. I wouldn't have thought to try that, but basmati does have a nice flavor.

SERVES 8

> 3 tablespoons olive oil
> 2 regular or turkey andouille sausages (about 12 ounces),
>   cut into bite-sized pieces (see Sources, page 267)
> 1 large onion, chopped
> 2 celery stalks, chopped
> 8 garlic cloves, minced or passed through a garlic press
> 2 cups (1 pound) dried red beans, sorted, rinsed, and drained
> ¼ cup chopped fresh parsley
> Leaves from 8 sprigs fresh thyme
> 1 bay leaf
> 1 tablespoon salt
> ½ teaspoon black pepper
> ¼ teaspoon baking soda
> Cooked white rice
> Hot sauce

1. In a large Dutch oven or heavy pot, warm the oil over medium-high heat. Add the sausage and sauté for 2 to 3 minutes. Add the onion, celery, and garlic and sauté for 3 to 5 minutes more.
2. Pour 6 cups water into the pot and add the beans, parsley, thyme, bay leaf, salt, black pepper, and baking soda. Cover and bring to a boil. Reduce the heat and simmer, covered, for 1½ to 2 hours, or until the beans are tender, stirring every 20 minutes or so. The beans can be made up to 3 days in advance and cooled, covered, and refrigerated, then reheated for serving.
3. To serve, divide the rice among eight bowls and pour the beans over the rice. Serve with hot sauce on the side.

Homemade Chicken Broth

The rule in my family is "don't ever throw away bones." I got in major trouble one time when my mom saw me tossing out some old chicken bones. "Why are you throwing away those perfectly good bones?" she demanded. I said, "Because I'm done with them," and she said, "You can make broth out of that!" Mom's right that everything's better with some fresh broth—it's tastier than store-bought, less salty, and can be frozen for months.

MAKES 3 QUARTS

3 pounds leftover chicken parts and bones, or 6 boneless,
 skinless chicken breast halves
4 celery stalks, chopped
1 large onion, chopped
1 tablespoon salt
1 teaspoon black pepper

1. In a stockpot over medium heat combine 10 cups water, the chicken, celery, onion, salt, and pepper. Bring to a boil, lower the heat, and simmer for 45 minutes. Taste and add a little more salt and pepper if desired.
2. Remove the chicken and, if using the breasts, reserve for another use, such as cornbread dressing (page 174). Use immediately, or let cool, then cover and refrigerate for up to 2 days or freeze for up to 3 months.

Homemade Vegetable Broth

Whenever you're cooking with a lot of vegetables, save any good trimmings to make broth. You can strain this for a smooth clear broth, but I like it a little chunky. It's up to you.

MAKES 2½ QUARTS

> 10 sprigs fresh flat-leaf parsley
> Leafy tops from 3 celery stalks plus 3 celery stalks, chopped
> 6 sprigs thyme
> 3 bay leaves
> 1 large onion, chopped
> 3 garlic cloves, chopped
> 2 (15-ounce) cans peeled plum tomatoes, roughly chopped
> 2 carrots, chopped
> 1 small leek, chopped

1. Use kitchen twine to tie the parsley, celery tops, thyme, and bay leaves in a bundle (or tie them up in cheesecloth). Place the herbs in a large stockpot with the celery, onion, garlic, and 4 quarts water.
2. Bring the stock to a boil and simmer for 30 minutes. Remove the herbs and add the tomatoes, carrots, and leek. Simmer for another 30 to 40 minutes.
3. Strain out the solids if you want a clear broth. Keep warm if using immediately, or let cool, then cover and keep in the refrigerator for up to 3 days or in the freezer for up to 3 months.

CHAPTER 4

Fish
and Shellfish

Fishing on the Bayou

When I was little, it always seemed like wherever we went fishing out on the swampy bayou, there was something ominous lurking.

The first order of business was keeping a close eye out for water moccasins. They're deadly poisonous, and my mother was always afraid because they hang out in the bushes and trees right above the water. They are also pretty smart—they wait over the areas where the white perch are and when the perch surface to catch bugs, the snakes drop down and get the fish. When my grandpa Ford used to work as a fishing tour guide, that's how he knew where to find the fish. He'd keep his eyes out for snakes up in the trees and stop the boat right there.

Once, when my mom and dad were out fishing, a snake fell right into their boat. My dad quickly tossed it out, but during the scuffle he ended up in the water, too! Well, he scrambled right back in, turned on the motor, and sped away down the bayou. When they stopped, my mom turned around and saw a water moccasin right behind them. "Charles," she said, thinking that the same snake had somehow kept pace, "you didn't go far enough!"

As crazy and dangerous as a Louisiana fishing trip might seem, getting to eat those delicious freshly caught perch was definitely worth the trouble.

Mama's Tuna Boats

If you're not into fried foods, you can easily adapt this recipe. Instead of frying them, roll teaspoonfuls of the tuna in plain dried bread crumbs to coat and place them in a pan brushed or sprayed lightly with oil. Bake for 25 to 30 minutes at 350 degrees F. To finish, I like to brown them under the broiler.

⁂ *Mom Says:* Faith always got excited when I made these; I think it was partly because that's one of the few times I'd make French fries as a side dish. Even if you don't serve them with fries you'll find that most kids love these bite-sized boats.

MAKES ABOUT 15 BOATS, SERVING 6 AS AN APPETIZER

Vegetable oil, for frying
1 (6-ounce) can tuna, drained
1 small onion, finely chopped
1 large egg
2 tablespoons plus 1 teaspoon all-purpose flour
1 teaspoon baking powder
1 teaspoon salt

1. Pour at least 2 inches of oil into a deep skillet, wok, or electric fryer and heat to about 375 degrees F. (If you don't have a thermometer, sprinkle in some flour. It should sizzle immediately.)
2. In a bowl, combine the tuna, onion, egg, flour, baking powder, and salt and mix well with a fork.
3. Drop the tuna mixture by heaping teaspoonfuls into the oil, working in batches if necessary to avoid overcrowding. The tuna boats will puff up and float as they cook. Fry them until they are deeply golden on one side, then turn the boats over (most will turn themselves over in the oil as they brown, but some need coaxing) and fry until golden on that side, too, about 3 minutes per boat. Use a slotted spoon or skimmer to transfer the boats to a paper towel–lined plate as they are ready. Serve hot.

Crab Cakes on Avocado, Tomato, and Arugula Salad

I grew up in the land-locked part of Louisiana, so I didn't have crab cakes until I was older and visited New Orleans. I was sold on them with my first bite! When I moved to New York I'd go to the Maryland Crab House for my crab cake fix. The secret of a great crab cake is to use fresh lump crabmeat from your favorite fish market or the specialty fish section in many of the larger supermarkets. Fresh is so much sweeter and more succulent than what you get from a can. I don't like a lot of breading, so I use crushed cornflakes—just enough to crisp the outside and hold the cake together. Served over a salad with avocado, tomato, and arugula, it's one of the best summer meals I know!

➸ *Mom Says:* You can freeze leftover cakes. Just store them flat in a freezer bag.

**MAKES 8 CAKES, SERVING 8 AS AN APPETIZER
OR 4 AS A MAIN COURSE**

4 tablespoons vegetable oil
½ cup chopped onion
2 tablespoons chopped red bell pepper
3 garlic cloves, minced or passed through a garlic press
1½ pounds fresh or frozen lump crabmeat (thawed and
    drained well if using frozen)
⅓ cup light or regular mayonnaise
2 scallions, chopped
1 large egg
3 tablespoons plain dried bread crumbs
2 tablespoons finely chopped dill pickle
2 tablespoons chopped fresh dill
1½ tablespoons Dijon mustard
1 teaspoon bottled horseradish, drained
¼ teaspoon cayenne pepper, or to taste
1½ cups crushed cornflakes

2 bunches arugula (about 8 cups)
1 large ripe tomato, cored and sliced
1 avocado, sliced
1 recipe Basil Balsamic Dressing (page 39)

1. In a nonstick frying pan over medium-high heat, warm 2 tablespoons of the oil. Add the onion, bell pepper, and garlic and sauté for 3 to 5 minutes, until wilted. Set aside.
2. In a medium bowl, combine the crab, mayonnaise, scallions, egg, bread crumbs, dill pickle, fresh dill, mustard, horseradish, and cayenne and mix well.
3. Form eight ³⁄₄-inch-thick crab cakes (about ⅓ cup each). Coat each with cornflake crumbs and place on a plate. Crab cakes can be covered and refrigerated for up to 1 day.
4. In a nonstick skillet over medium heat, warm 1 tablespoon oil. Add 4 of the crab cakes and brown on both sides, 5 to 7 minutes each. Remove to a plate and cover with foil to keep warm until ready to serve. Add the remaining tablespoon oil and cook the remaining crab cakes.
5. Arrange the arugula on serving plates. Add some tomato and avocado slices and drizzle with some of the dressing. Place a warm crab cake on top and serve immediately.

Jay Chevalier, a family friend and fellow Louisianan,
and me eating our local treasure, crawfish.

Salmon Cakes with Dill Pickle Tartar Sauce

This recipe is a spin-off of my mother's tuna boat recipe (page 77) but I sauté these cakes instead of deep-frying them. Although I prefer to use fresh salmon, canned is great in a pinch, and will work just as well. If you like, you can form the salmon cakes up to a day in advance and keep them in the refrigerator until you're ready to cook them.

MAKES 6 CAKES, SERVING 6 AS AN APPETIZER OR 2 AS A MAIN COURSE

Dill Pickle Tartar Sauce

> 1 cup light or regular mayonnaise
> ½ cup nonfat yogurt
> ⅓ cup dill pickle relish or chopped dill pickles
> 1 tablespoon chopped fresh dill
> 1 teaspoon Dijon mustard

In a small bowl, whisk together all the ingredients. Cover and chill until ready to serve or overnight.

Salmon Cakes

> 1½ pounds cooked or raw skinless salmon fillet, or 2 (15-ounce) cans salmon
> 1 cup plus 2 tablespoons plain dried bread crumbs
> ¼ cup Dill Pickle Tartar Sauce (see above)
> 2 scallions, chopped
> 1 large egg, slightly beaten
> 1 tablespoon Dijon mustard
> 1 tablespoon chopped fresh dill
> 2 teaspoons capers, drained
> 1 garlic clove, minced or passed through a garlic press
> 4 tablespoons vegetable oil

1. If you are using raw salmon, rinse it and pat dry. Place the fillet in a steamer basket or metal pot insert for a large pot. Fill the pot with 1 inch of water, making sure the water does not come up to the level of the basket, and put the basket into the pot. Steam over high heat for 10 to 15 minutes, until the fish is light pink and flaky. Do not overcook. (If you are using canned salmon, check for and remove any large bones.)

2. To make the salmon cakes, in a medium bowl, put the salmon, the 2 tablespoons bread crumbs, tartar sauce, scallions, egg, mustard, dill, capers, and garlic and mix well. Form six ¾-inch-thick cakes using about ½ cup of the mixture per cake. Coat the cakes with the remaining cup bread crumbs and place them on a plate. Salmon cakes can be covered and refrigerated for up to 1 day or wrapped well and frozen for up to 1 month. Defrost before proceeding.

3. In a nonstick frying pan over medium-high heat, warm 2 tablespoons of the oil. Place 3 of the cakes in the pan and cook on both sides until brown, 2 to 3 minutes per side. Remove to a plate and cover with foil to keep warm. Add the remaining 2 tablespoons oil to the pan and cook the remaining cakes. Serve immediately with tartar sauce on the side.

All-you-can-peel-and-eat
crawfish!

Southern-Style Fried Catfish

My Grandpa Walker used to say about catfish, "If you can't catch 'em yourself, then you don't deserve to eat 'em."

Since I love catfish, I was always motivated to help him catch them. Now my grandpa didn't have a lot of time to fish. He had a farm and was a Baptist preacher. So to catch the catfish, twice a week or more he laid out trotlines on the river near his house. When the time came to pull them up, well, that's where I came in. I would hold the boat steady while he pulled.

You had to be careful when pulling up those lines, though. You never knew what you'd get. Occasionally you'd pull up a snake or a turtle! Mostly, though, there'd be catfish in all sizes, some up to four feet long! If you were lucky, you'd get a white perch or a bass on the line and that would be a real prize. You just never knew.

To have catfish the way you'd have them at a fried fish stand down South, serve them with French fries, hush puppies, coleslaw, pickles, lemon wedges, and catsup, or serve them with Cora's Creamy Country Potato Salad (page 41), field peas or black-eyed peas, and Dill Pickle Tartar Sauce (page 80).

SERVES 6

> Peanut oil, for frying
> 6 skinless catfish fillets (6 to 8 ounces each), rinsed and patted dry
> Salt and black pepper
> 1½ cups yellow cornmeal
> 1 lemon, cut into 6 wedges

1. Pour at least 2 inches of oil into a deep skillet, wok, or electric fryer and heat to about 375 degrees F. (If you don't have a thermometer, sprinkle in some cornmeal. It should sizzle immediately.)
2. Line a platter with paper towels. Divide each fillet in half lengthwise and lay the fish on a baking sheet. Season with salt and pepper on both sides.
3. Place the cornmeal in a lidded container or resealable plastic bag. Put a few pieces of fish in the bag or container and, holding it closed, shake well to coat the fish. Return the fish to the baking sheet and repeat with the remaining pieces.

4. Use tongs to lower a piece of fish into the oil. If it sinks, the oil is not hot enough—wait until the first piece has risen and begun to sizzle before adding more pieces. Avoid overcrowding or the oil will get too cool.

5. Turn the fillets when they are golden on the bottom and cook until both sides are golden brown, 5 to 7 minutes total. When they're done, the fillets will float freely and the fish inside will be white and flaky. Transfer the fillets to the paper towel–lined platter as they are done. Serve hot, with lemon wedges.

Grandpa Larry Walker and his dog in the
boat we used to set trotlines on the river.

Oven-Fried Pecan-Crusted Catfish

My version of fried catfish, made in the oven, is just as crispy as my mom's, thanks to the pecans and Grape-Nuts cereal, but uses a lot less oil. I serve this with a salad made from bitter greens, like the Arugula Salad with Honey-Mustard Dressing (page 34), or even a simple salad of field greens.

SERVES 8

1 tablespoon vegetable or olive oil
8 skinless catfish fillets (6 to 8 ounces each), rinsed and patted dry
1½ teaspoons Faith's Special Seasoning (page 266) or
    Cajun seasoning (see Sources, page 267)
3 large egg whites
1 tablespoon Dijon mustard
1 cup crushed cornflakes
½ cup finely chopped toasted pecans (see page 244)
½ cup yellow cornmeal
¼ cup Grape-Nuts cereal
Dill Pickle Tartar Sauce (page 80)

1. Preheat the oven to 450 degrees F. Brush a rimmed baking sheet with the oil.
2. Season the catfish fillets on both sides with Faith's seasoning.
3. In a bowl, whisk together the egg whites and mustard. In another bowl, mix together the cornflake crumbs, pecans, cornmeal, and Grape-Nuts.
4. Dip each fillet in the egg white mixture, then coat it with the cereal mixture and place it on the baking sheet.
5. Bake for 15 to 20 minutes, until golden brown on the outside and white and flaky in the middle. Serve hot with tartar sauce.

Cajun Better'n Blackened Catfish

The first cookbook I got when I moved to Los Angeles was by Paul Prudhomme, and it was inspirational. When I went to visit him at his restaurant, he told me that his blackened catfish was actually the result of a mistake his mom made once. She accidentally let the fish get a bit burnt, then added a whole lot of seasoning to cover it up. It was an instant hit in his family, and he went on to make it famous.

I like my fish on the cusp of burnt—crispy and flavorful, but browned, rather than blackened. Making sure your pan is hot enough will guarantee that the fish cooks through. This recipe will also work with other firm fish like cod, halibut, mahi mahi, or grouper.

I like to serve this dish with Dilled Rice with Corn and Garlic (page 172). I grew up on dill and it is always great with fish. It grows like a weed in Louisiana, but out here in my Los Angeles garden it doesn't do so well. It'll get to a certain height, then something eats it. At least I can always find it at the grocery store!

SERVES 6

> 2 tablespoons sweet paprika
> 4 teaspoons black pepper
> 1 tablespoon salt
> 1 teaspoon dried thyme
> ¼ teaspoon cayenne pepper
> 6 skinless catfish fillets (6 to 8 ounces each), rinsed and patted dry
> 3 tablespoons olive oil
> 3 tablespoons butter

1. In a small bowl, mix together the paprika, black pepper, salt, thyme, and cayenne. Sprinkle the seasoning over both sides of each fillet (about 2 teaspoons per ½-pound fillet) and rub in.
2. In a large cast-iron skillet over medium-high heat, warm the oil and melt the butter. Place 2 fillets in the skillet, cover, and cook for about 5 minutes on each side, until the fish is flaky and browned on the outside. Transfer the cooked fillets to a platter and keep them warm while repeating the process with the remaining fish. Serve hot.

Broiled Red Snapper with Olives, Onions, and Tomatoes

When I moved to New York, I had fish that wasn't breaded and fried for the first time in my life. My boyfriend at the time owned a deli, and the cook there made broiled sole. I thought it was just delicious. I quickly learned how to prepare fish in lots of different ways: broiled, baked, sautéed, and poached. Then I applied those methods to my favorite fish from home, snapper and catfish.

Early in my career I spent a few weeks in the former Yugoslavia, making a movie. The cook on the set used to take tomatoes and onions, chop them up, and put them on top of fish and then broil it. This is my version of that amazingly simple recipe. My one big change was to add olives. Leave them out if you don't like them.

SERVES 4

3 tablespoons olive oil
½ small red onion, chopped
1 small tomato, seeded and chopped
¼ cup chopped pitted kalamata or niçoise olives
4 red snapper fillets (about 8 ounces each), skin on,
    rinsed and patted dry
1 teaspoon salt
½ teaspoon black pepper
½ teaspoon hot chili powder
2 tablespoons butter
1 lemon, quartered

1. Preheat the broiler. Prepare a broiling pan by lining it with foil and coating it with 2 tablespoons of the oil. Fold up the edges of the foil to hold in the juices.
2. In a small nonstick pan over high heat, warm the remaining tablespoon oil. Add the onion and sauté for 2 minutes, until it turns translucent around the edges. In a small bowl, toss the onion with the tomato and olives. Set aside.
3. Season both sides of the fillets with salt, pepper, and chili powder, patting them with

some of the oil on the foil. Place them in the broiling pan and spread the onion mixture evenly on top of the fillets; dot each with butter.

4. Place the fillets under the broiler for about 10 minutes, until the fish flakes with a fork. Do not overcook. Serve with lemon wedges on the side.

Gone fishin' with Mom.

Dilled Grilled Salmon Niçoise with Zesty Lemon-Herb Dressing

This dish has tiny green beans cooked just enough to keep their crunch, salty olives, ripe tomatoes, greens, red potatoes, and grilled salmon that has been marinating in a citrus dressing with a touch of honey. It's the perfect light supper but it's also colorful and elegant enough to serve to company, especially in the summer.

SERVES 4

Salmon and Lemon-Herb Dressing

⅔ cup olive oil

¼ cup freshly squeezed lemon juice (from about 2 lemons)

2 scallions, chopped

1 tablespoon chopped fresh dill

1 garlic clove, minced or passed through a garlic press

1 teaspoon Dijon mustard

¾ teaspoon salt

½ teaspoon black pepper

½ teaspoon honey

1½ pounds salmon fillet, skin on, rinsed and patted dry

In a bowl, whisk together all dressing ingredients. Place the salmon in a large shallow dish. Pour ¼ cup of the dressing over the fish. Cover and let marinate in the refrigerator for at least 1 hour or up to 4 hours. Reserve the remaining dressing for the salad.

Salad

¾ pound haricots verts or thin, small string beans

8 small red potatoes (about ¾ pound), halved or quartered if large

2 heads butter lettuce

3 tomatoes, cut into wedges

½ cup pitted kalamata or niçoise olives

Fresh dill

1. Fill a medium saucepan halfway with salted water and bring to a boil over high heat. Fill a medium bowl halfway with cold water and ice cubes and set aside. Plunge the beans into the boiling water and blanch for 3 minutes. Use a slotted spoon to transfer them immediately to the ice water bath to stop the cooking. Return the water to a boil and add the potatoes. Cook the potatoes for 12 to 15 minutes, until tender. Drain and chill in the ice water bath. Drain the chilled beans and potatoes.

2. Light the grill or preheat a stovetop grill over high heat for 5 minutes. Grill the marinated salmon in an outdoor grill, covered, or on the stovetop grill, until just done (light pink inside and out), about 5 minutes per side.

3. To assemble the salad, arrange a bed of lettuce leaves on each of four plates. Arrange the chilled beans and tomatoes in an outer ring with the potatoes inside. Peel the skin off the grilled salmon and chunk the meat. Place the warm salmon chunks on top of the potatoes. Garnish with olives, pour on the dressing to taste, and sprinkle some fresh dill on top.

Me (in the red hooded shirt), my sister, Devon (across from me),
and two college friends sit down for some crawfish.

Cousin Sue's Quick
Shrimp Etouffée

My mom's cousin, Sue, is a terrific cook. She's traveled a lot, and so, like me, she's had a lot of different influences on her cooking. This recipe is pretty traditional except for one key thing: Sue uses the microwave to make the roux. It's faster and easier than the usual method of standing over the pot stirring. When she can get crawfish she'll use those, but shrimp are great, too. Sue serves her etouffée over rice with oven-toasted garlic-buttered French bread and a crispy green salad.

⁂ **Mom Says:** Sue Walker is married to my first cousin, Carman Walker. She is a retired social worker known for her kind heart and helpfulness in Jonesville, the small town where I grew up and where we were living when Faith was born. Sue does the most beautiful weddings, anniversary celebrations, and country club occasions that she calls "putting on a do." Over the years she's collected a wide selection of lace tablecloths, table skirts, silver and crystal serving pieces, candelabra, lattices, and arches, as well as more than a few delicious recipes.

SERVES 12

Vegetable Puree
> 1 cup chopped celery
> 1 cup chopped scallions
> 1 cup chopped bell pepper
> 1 cup chopped white onion
> 1 stick butter

Put the celery, scallions, bell pepper, onion, and butter in a large microwave-proof dish. Cover and microwave on high for 5 minutes, then remove and stir. Cover and microwave again until soft enough to puree, another 2 minutes. Transfer to a blender and puree.

Roux

²/₃ cup vegetable oil

²/₃ cup all-purpose flour

In another microwave-proof dish, stir together the oil and flour and microwave on high for 6 minutes to make a light brown, toasty-smelling roux. You can also make the roux in the traditional way: Warm the oil in a small saucepan set over medium-low heat. Stir in the flour and cook, stirring, until the roux becomes fragrant and light brown, 20 to 30 minutes.

Broth and Shrimp

6 (14-ounce) cans chicken broth, or 10 cups homemade (page 72)

2 (15-ounce) cans diced tomatoes

1 (6-ounce) can tomato paste

¹/₂ teaspoon crab boil

Salt to taste

3 pounds peeled and deveined shrimp or crawfish

Cooked white rice

While the roux cooks, pour the chicken broth into a large pot and bring it to a simmer. Pour the vegetable puree and roux into the hot chicken broth and stir well. Add the diced tomatoes, tomato paste, and crab boil and simmer for 15 minutes. Taste and add salt if desired. Stir in the shrimp or crawfish, cover, and simmer for another 10 minutes. Remove the pot from the heat and let it stand, covered, for 5 to 10 minutes. Serve over the hot cooked rice.

Aunt Brenda's Shrimp Sauté

When my mom and Aunt Brenda were little girls, people sometimes wouldn't think they were sisters. Brenda has dark hair and dark eyes, the exact opposite of my mother, who is blond with blue eyes. Since they were the only children in the family, they were very close and still are. Aunt Brenda lives two hours away from mom, and if they don't see each other as often as they want to, they sure talk on the phone a lot.

One thing they have in common is that they're both great cooks. Aunt Brenda comes up with things that my mom would never think of, like this quick shrimp dish. When Aunt Brenda sent her recipe for this book, my mother was so happy because she remembered eating it at Aunt Brenda's house and thinking "this is so good!" The only changes I've made to her recipe are to use my own seasoning mix instead of store-bought Cajun seasoning and to add fresh herbs.

SERVES 4

> 8 tablespoons (1 stick) butter
> 4 garlic cloves, minced or passed through a garlic press
> 2 pounds medium shrimp, peeled and deveined
> 2 to 3 teaspoons Faith's Special Seasoning (page 266) or
>   Cajun seasoning (see Sources, page 267)
> 1 teaspoon salt
> ½ teaspoon black pepper
> 3 tablespoons chopped fresh herbs such as parsley, basil, chives, or thyme
> 1 to 2 tablespoons freshly squeezed lemon juice, to taste

1. In a sauté pan over medium-high heat, melt the butter. Add the garlic and sauté for 2 to 3 minutes.
2. Add the shrimp, Faith's seasoning, salt, and pepper. Reduce the heat to medium and sauté, tossing, until the shrimp start to turn pink, about 2 minutes. Raise the heat to high and cook off any liquid from the shrimp, about 1 minute more. Do not overcook. Add the herbs and lemon juice, toss, and serve.

CHAPTER 5

Poultry

Southern Fried Chicken

Fried chicken is one of the ultimate Southern meals, and we ate it fairly often when I was a kid. We liked it best served very hot, right out of the pan, so the outside was still crispy and the insides steamy. My mother absolutely expected us to be sitting at the table ready to eat when the chicken was done frying. Otherwise . . . well, let's just say my mother was skilled at getting us to sit down and stay there. And trust me, we always did.

⚜ *Mom Says:* When I taught at South Alexandria Primary School, one evening we teachers were discussing what we could fix for our families' supper, and the discussion turned to fried chicken. We were all young mothers and had not yet perfected the art of getting the chicken done through. An older lady who worked at the school told us to get a heavy Dutch oven, pour in oil and get it sizzling hot, test the temperature with a pinch of flour, then poke all the chicken down in the grease and pop the lid on. We all said at once, "Pop the lid on?!!" She said, "Yes! If you want tender, crispy chicken all done clear through, you just try it." Well, I went right by the store, bought a fresh chicken, took it home, and tried it. I couldn't believe it, but it worked. Now I always use her method and think of her.

This particular recipe doesn't call for a heavy batter, and I like it better that way. The chicken should never be soggy and grease-logged, and the batter is often the greasiest part, so a thin coating of flour, salt, and pepper (or sometimes I use Cajun seasoning for a spicy taste) suits me fine. Frying is an art—as is getting everybody to the table in time to serve it hot!

SERVES 4

 1 to 2 quarts vegetable oil
 1 chicken (3½ pounds), cut into 8 pieces (or use an equivalent
  amount of all white- or all dark-meat pieces)
 Salt and pepper
 1 to 1½ cups all-purpose flour

1. Fill a heavy Dutch oven or a deep-fryer one-third full of oil and set over medium-high heat.
2. Rinse and drain, but do not dry the chicken. Season on all sides with salt and pepper.

3. Place 1 cup flour in a plastic bowl with a tight-sealing cover or in a paper bag. Add a few pieces of chicken to the flour, close the lid or bag, then shake vigorously until the chicken is completely coated. Repeat, adding more flour as needed, until all the chicken is floured. (Alternatively, simply dredge the chicken pieces in a bowl of flour.)

4. The oil is ready for frying when it has reached a temperature of 350 degrees F. If you don't have a deep-fry or candy thermometer, add a pinch of flour to the hot oil. If it sizzles, the oil is ready.

5. Using tongs, add the first piece of chicken. The oil around the chicken should sizzle. If the chicken appears to just lie there, wait until it starts to sizzle, then add all the other pieces, pushing them down into the hot oil. The oil should come up and surround the chicken, but if a tip or two is out of the oil, don't worry. Cover the pot immediately and let the chicken cook for 10 minutes (if the pot seems to be bubbling too furiously, lower the heat to medium).

6. Uncover the pot and, using tongs, lift the bottom pieces and check for brownness. This allows other pieces to take the bottom spots. Continue cooking uncovered until all the pieces are crisp and golden brown and the juices run clear when pricked with a knife, about 5 minutes. They will be crispy, yet tender and done throughout. Drain in a pan layered with paper towels. Serve immediately.

Golden Crispy Oven-Fried Chicken

My husband, Campion, doesn't usually like to eat fried chicken, but there used to be a place in the San Fernando Valley that made great broasted chicken. They used a hot-hot-hot oven, and the heat would basically fry the chicken in the fat from its skin. When that place closed I thought, "I've got to learn how to make this at home." And it wasn't until a few years ago, when I was talking to one of my friends from back in Louisiana, that I learned oven-fried chicken is nothing new. They did it in our church for big gatherings when they didn't want people standing over a fryer. It was a lot neater and cleaner and nearly as delicious.

I use skinless chicken because I don't want the extra fat, but that makes it more challenging to get the chicken crisp—make sure you have the chicken coated with crumbs. I like to use a combination of bread crumbs and cornflakes because those crunchy cornflakes give the chicken a nice golden crust.

SERVES 4 TO 5

> 1 chicken (3½ pounds), cut into 10 pieces (breast quartered),
>   skin removed
> 2 tablespoons plus 2 teaspoons Faith's Special Seasoning (page 266) or
>   Cajun seasoning (see Sources, page 267)
> 1 cup buttermilk
> 1 tablespoon freshly squeezed lemon juice
> 1 teaspoon grated lemon zest
> Olive oil, for brushing or spraying
> 1½ cups crushed cornflakes
> 1 cup plain dried bread crumbs

1. Rinse the chicken and pat it dry with paper towels. Rub the 2 tablespoons Faith's seasoning onto the chicken and place it in a marinating dish. Whisk together the buttermilk, lemon juice, and lemon zest. Pour the mixture over the chicken, cover the dish, and let marinate in the refrigerator for at least 30 minutes, or overnight.
2. Preheat the oven to 400 degrees F. Coat a large baking pan with olive oil.

3. In a wide, shallow bowl, combine the cornflakes, bread crumbs, and the 2 teaspoons of Faith's seasoning. Roll each piece of chicken in the crumbs, pressing them onto the chicken to make sure the coating adheres well.

4. Place the chicken in the prepared baking pan, leaving a small space between each piece. Spray or drizzle the chicken pieces lightly with olive oil and bake for 20 minutes. Rotate the pan and spray or drizzle again with olive oil. Bake for 20 more minutes, until the juices run clear. Serve hot.

Crispy Oven-Fried Chicken Breasts

This is a simplified, boneless version of Golden Crispy Oven-Fried Chicken (page 96), which is perfect for kids. If you have little ones in the house, put them to work here; they love crushing the cornflakes to bits! Wrap the cornflakes in wax paper, place them on a rimmed baking sheet (to lessen the mess), and hand 'em a rolling pin. Then stand back . . .

If you are serving this to kids, they will enjoy dunking pieces of the chicken breast into the Honey-Mustard Dipping Sauce on page 22. I like to arrange the chicken over a field green salad dressed with a tangy lemon dressing (see page 88). But it's also great served just plain with your favorite side dish.

SERVES 4

> 4 boneless, skinless chicken breast halves (about 1½ pounds)
> 3 teaspoons Faith's Special Seasoning (page 266) or
>   Cajun seasoning (see Sources, page 267), or to taste
> 1 cup buttermilk
> 2 tablespoons Dijon mustard
> 1½ cups crushed cornflakes
> Salt and black pepper

1. Rinse the chicken breasts, pat them dry, and place them in a marinating dish. Sprinkle all sides of the chicken with 2 teaspoons Faith's seasoning. Whisk the buttermilk and mustard together in a small bowl and pour the mixture over the chicken. Cover and let marinate in the refrigerator for at least an hour or overnight, but no longer.
2. Preheat the oven to 350 degrees F.
3. Season the cornflake crumbs with the remaining teaspoon Faith's seasoning and salt and pepper to taste. Place the mixture in a large shallow bowl or resealable plastic bag. Add the chicken pieces to the bowl or bag and shake to coat each piece with crumbs. Arrange the coated pieces on a baking dish.
4. Bake for 30 to 40 minutes, until crispy and golden brown and the juices run clear when the meat is pierced with a fork. Slice if desired and serve immediately.

Saturday Night Chicken Sausage and Cabbage Sauté

Sautéing cabbage quickly doesn't let it cook down much and keeps it crunchy, which I love. I use chicken sausage because I like the flavor with cabbage, but you can use turkey or pork as well. Serve with Red-Hot Black-Eyed Peas (page 158), potatoes, or brown rice.

SERVES 6

> 2 tablespoons olive oil
> 2 (12-ounce) packages chicken sausage, sliced in thirds
> 1 large red onion, chopped
> 3 carrots, peeled and cut into ½-inch chunks
> 3 stalks celery, cut into ½- or 1-inch pieces
> 1½ teaspoons caraway seeds
> ½ teaspoon crushed red pepper flakes
> 2 tablespoons soy sauce
> ¼ teaspoon sugar
> 1 small green cabbage, shredded (about 8 cups)
> Salt

1. Heat the olive oil in a large Dutch oven or stockpot over medium-high heat. Add the sausage and brown it on all sides, then lower the heat to medium and cook for 5 minutes, stirring occasionally, until the sausage is browned. Transfer the sausage to a plate and set aside.

2. Add the onion, celery, carrots, caraway seeds, and red pepper flakes to the pot and sauté for 1 minute. In a small dish, stir together the soy sauce and sugar. Add the cabbage to the pot in three batches, drizzling with the soy mixture and stirring after each addition, until all the soy mixture is added and the cabbage is well coated.

3. Add the sausage to the pot, cover, and let steam for 3 to 4 minutes. The cabbage will be crisp-steamed. If you like, you can sauté it for a few more minutes, until done to taste, but don't let it go too far, or it will shrink down to nothing! Serve immediately.

Dinner-on-the-Ground Chicken 'n' Dumplin's

As the granddaughter of a Baptist preacher, one of my fondest childhood memories was attending church dinners "on the ground." The women of the church would bring their favorite family dishes and spread them out on tables under the shade trees outside after Sunday service.

Grandma Cora's signature all-time favorite dish was a big pot of homemade chicken and dumplings. The only catch was, you had to get to them before everyone else! I can still hear Grandma's voice as she stood there guarding her dumplings during the blessing. "Faithie, c'mon. You better get over here and get some of these dumplin's. They're gonna be gone!" I'd slide in next to her, holding up my plate with a smile from ear to ear. "Gimme some, Grandma! I want two spoonfuls!" She'd give me three just to be safe.

Make sure to prepare the dumplings at least a half hour before you plan to cook them. My grandmother always said that these dumplings taste better when you freeze them first, or you can just put them in the refrigerator for an hour. Don't expect fluffy, thick dumplings—these are thin and delicate, almost like noodles. You roll them out in a lot of flour, which not only helps keep them from sticking together, but also thickens the broth.

SERVES 6

Dumplings

> 2 cups all-purpose flour, plus ½ cup for rolling out dumplings
> 1 teaspoon salt
> ¼ teaspoon baking powder
> 2 tablespoons unsalted butter, chilled
> 1 large egg, lightly beaten
> ½ cup milk

1. In a food processor or in a large bowl, pulse or whisk together the 2 cups flour and the salt and baking powder. Pulse the butter into the dry ingredients or cut it in using a pastry cutter or two knives, until the mixture resembles coarse meal.

2. In a small bowl, beat together the egg and milk. Gradually add this mixture to the dry ingredients, pulsing or using a fork to mix the ingredients a little at a time, just until a dough is formed. Do not overmix.

3. Divide the dough into two balls. Liberally dust a work surface with the ½ cup flour and roll out each ball as thin as possible, using more flour as needed (no more than ⅛ inch thick). Cut the dough into 1½-inch squares and place them on flour-coated wax paper. Air dry the uncooked dumplings for at least 30 minutes (or wrap them well and freeze for up to a month; defrost overnight in the refrigerator before cooking), or refrigerate them, uncovered, for 1 hour.

Chicken and Broth

1 chicken (about 3½ pounds), cut into 8 pieces
4 celery stalks, chopped
1 medium onion, chopped
Salt and black pepper

1. Rinse the chicken. In a large stockpot over medium heat, put 3 quarts water along with the chicken, celery, onion, ½ teaspoon salt, and ¼ teaspoon pepper. Bring to a boil, then lower the heat and simmer, uncovered, until the chicken is tender and cooked through, 30 to 40 minutes. Transfer the chicken to a board and let cool for a few minutes. Skim any foam from the broth, add additional salt to taste, and set aside in the stockpot.

2. When the meat is cool enough to handle, pull the chicken meat off the bones and set aside. Place the bones, 1 quart water, ½ teaspoon salt, and ¼ teaspoon pepper in a smaller pot and boil for 40 minutes, skimming any foam. Strain the liquid and reserve to add to the chicken and dumplings when reheating.

3. Bring the mixture in the stockpot to a rolling boil. Add the dumplings a few at a time, letting the broth return to a rolling boil before each addition. Once all the dumplings are in the pot, simmer them for 5 minutes, stirring once or twice.

4. Add the chicken and and simmer for another 10 minutes, separating any dumplings that stick together. Remove from the heat and let the chicken and dumplings sit for about 20 minutes before serving. Taste and add more salt and pepper if desired. Reheat—adding the additional reserved liquid as needed—before serving.

Ragin' Cajun Roasted Chickens

I'm from central Louisiana and our way of cooking is different from Cajun cuisine. We usually brown things rather than blacken them, and there's crawfish, but people where I come from don't suck on the heads like they do farther south. We don't have people eating alligator up in our neck of the woods, either. They've been known to try it, but it's not a mainstay. Our food is still very flavorful, but we usually hold back on red pepper, cayenne, and hot sauce. Hot sauce is out on the table, but not necessarily in the food.

Because of all the spices in this recipe, I think of it as my Cajun roasted chicken. The trick here is to rub the seasonings into the chicken and let it sit in the refrigerator overnight to soak up all that flavor. Baste a lot while you're roasting, so the skin gets crisp and delicious. Leftovers make amazing chicken sandwiches.

> ✤ *Mom Says:* Whenever I roast chicken or make pie I think it's more practical to make two at once. Faith and I have developed a lot of different ways to use up leftover roasted chicken or turn it into a second dinner. I tend to make chicken pot pies, while Faith will make some kind of pasta with chicken, or a chicken salad.

SERVES 8

2 whole chickens (about 3½ pounds each)
2 tablespoons sweet paprika
2 teaspoons salt
2 teaspoons black pepper
2 teaspoons Faith's Special Seasoning (page 266) or
    Cajun seasoning (see Sources, page 267)
½ teaspoon dried thyme
¼ teaspoon crushed red pepper flakes
3 tablespoons vegetable oil
2 celery stalks, chopped
1 green bell pepper, chopped
1 medium onion, chopped, and 1 large onion, sliced
10 garlic cloves, minced or passed through a garlic press
4 bay leaves

1. Rinse the chickens and pat them dry with paper towels. In a small bowl, mix together the paprika, salt, black pepper, Faith's seasoning, thyme, and crushed red pepper flakes. Coat the outside and inside of each chicken with 1½ tablespoons of this seasoning mix and reserve the remaining seasoning mix. Wrap the chicken in plastic and refrigerate for at least 1 hour or overnight.

2. Preheat the oven to 350 degrees F and place a large roasting pan in the oven to warm.

3. In a skillet over medium-high heat, warm 2 tablespoons of the oil. Add the celery, bell pepper, chopped onion, and garlic and sauté until tender, 5 to 7 minutes. Stir in the remaining seasoning mix and let cool. Puree in a food processor or finely chop by hand to make a coarse paste.

4. Carefully loosen the skin over the chicken breasts and stuff the vegetable paste between the skin and meat. Insert 1 bay leaf on each side of both chickens. Tie the legs together with string.

5. Add the remaining tablespoon of oil to the roasting pan and heat for 2 minutes in the oven. Take the preheated pan out of the oven and place it on the stovetop or on a large trivet. In the preheated pan, quickly brown the backs of the chickens for 1 minute, then the breast sides for 30 seconds. Arrange the onion slices on the bottom of the roasting pan and place the chickens, breast sides up, on top of the onions. The onions provide a cushion for the chickens and will brown while baking.

6. Roast the birds for 1 hour to 1 hour and 15 minutes, basting with the pan juices every 20 minutes and rotating the chickens as needed so that they cook evenly on all sides. The chickens are done when the meat is no longer pink at the thighbone (check by piercing with a small knife).

7. Transfer the roasted chickens to a serving platter and cover with foil to keep warm. Place the roasting pan with the onions on the stovetop over medium heat. Stir and simmer until the onions fall apart and the juices thicken, about 10 minutes. Add ½ cup water and salt to taste and simmer until it gets as thick as you like.

8. Carve and serve the chicken, spooning the gravy on top.

Faith's Chicken with Barbecue Salsa

My dad taught me how to barbecue. Like most men, he loves to grill, and barbecued chicken is one of his favorite dishes. He's really attentive to the chicken, turning and moving it so it doesn't get too brown before the center cooks through. My version is slightly different in that I put fresh salsa in the sauce. But like him, I only add the sauce toward the end of cooking the chicken. Use your favorite brand of barbecue sauce here. I like a hickory-flavored one.

SERVES 4

1 chicken (about 3½ pounds), cut into 8 pieces
4 tablespoons olive oil
1 tablespoon red wine vinegar
1 teaspoon Dijon mustard
Salt and black pepper
2 garlic cloves, chopped
1 cup chunky salsa, preferably fresh (from the prepared foods
   section of the grocery store), drained of excess liquid
2 cups (16 ounces) hickory-flavored barbecue sauce

1. Rinse the chicken, pat dry with paper towels, and arrange the pieces in a marinating dish. In a large bowl, whisk together 3 tablespoons of the olive oil with the vinegar, mustard, and salt and pepper to taste. Add the chicken pieces, turning to coat, cover, and let marinate in the refrigerator for at least ½ hour or overnight.

2. In a saucepan, warm the remaining tablespoon of olive oil over medium heat. Add the garlic and sauté until golden, but not brown, about 1 minute. Add the salsa, stir a few times, then pour in the barbecue sauce and cook for 5 minutes, stirring frequently.

3. Preheat or light the grill or preheat a broiler. When the coals are ashy gray, lay on the chicken, skin side up, or place the chicken in a broiler-safe pan and position it 5 inches from the heat source. Grill, covered, or broil for 10 minutes, then turn the

chicken and grill, covered, or broil skin side down, for another 10 minutes. Now flip the pieces again, brush the tops with some of the barbecue sauce, and grill, covered, or broil until the juices run clear when a piece of chicken is pierced with a small knife, about 10 minutes more. Serve, passing the remaining barbecue sauce at the table.

Grandma Cora and Grandpa Larry Walker at a church dinner on the ground. Grandma's famous chicken 'n' dumplin's (page 100) are in the pot in front of Grandpa.

Old-Fashioned Smothered Chicken

Smothered chicken is just an old tried-and-true formula. It's the simplest recipe but so good. I find eating my mother's smothered chicken on rice so comforting and soothing.

This recipe can be made with a whole chicken, or with all light or dark meat. But individual preference is the rule. If you make the dish ahead and chill it, you can skim the fat from the top before reheating and serving.

⚜ *Mom Says:* This chicken recipe is made in just one pot. I don't know if it's typically Southern, but it's typical of our family. I consider it a fricassee, but other people call it stewed chicken or simmered chicken. When Faith gave her friend Candice Bergen the recipe over the phone one day, Candice said it reminded her of something she had in France. So maybe it has a little bit of French influence.

SERVES 4

> 1 chicken (about 3½ pounds), cut into 10 pieces (breast quartered)
> 1 to 2 tablespoons Faith's Special Seasoning (page 266) or
>   Cajun seasoning (see Sources, page 267)
> 1 teaspoon salt
> ¼ cup vegetable oil
> 1 large onion, chopped
> 2 medium baking potatoes, peeled and cut into ½-inch chunks, optional
> 3 carrots, thickly sliced, optional
> ½ cup fresh or frozen green peas, optional
> 2 to 3 tablespoons chopped fresh herbs such as parsley,
>   basil, or cilantro, optional

1. Rinse the chicken pieces and pat dry with paper towels. Sprinkle all over with Faith's seasoning and salt.
2. In a Dutch oven or other heavy pot with a lid, warm the oil over high heat. Add the chicken and sear on all sides until browned, about 10 minutes. (If there is too much chicken for easy turning, sear half the pieces, then transfer them to a plate and sear

the other half.) Add the onion and push the pieces around and under the chicken so that the onion sears and begins to fall apart. It will take another 10 minutes to get everything nice and brown.

3. Add 2 cups water, ½ cup at a time. Let the liquid come to a simmer before adding more water each time. When the last of the water has been added and the juice is bubbling, reduce the heat to low and pop on the lid. Cook for 15 minutes, then turn the chicken in its juice. The pan liquid will not cover all the chicken completely, so rotate the top and bottom pieces at least once. Cook for another 30 to 45 minutes, until the chicken is tender. At this point, the chicken can be cooled, covered, and refrigerated for up to 1 day if desired. Reheat and serve; or if adding the optional vegetables, reheat until the liquid is simmering before continuing.

4. Add the potatoes, carrots, and peas and simmer, covered, until the vegetables are tender, about 15 minutes. Stir in the fresh herbs just before serving.

Chicken Breasts Stuffed with Mustard Green–Pecan Pesto

The first thing I learned to make in high school home economics class was a rolled stuffed chicken dish that we called chicken saltimbocca. You pounded the chicken breast and stuffed it with ham, tomatoes, and Swiss cheese, then you rolled it up, breaded it, and baked it. It was crispy outside, with melted cheese inside, and I thought, "Oh my God, this is the neatest thing"—I felt like a gourmet cook. Stuffed chicken breasts became one of the first meals I made for every boyfriend I ever had, and I'd adapt the recipe depending on what they liked to eat, making it nondairy for one boyfriend, or with corn and jalapeños for one from California. Recently, I tried it with a pesto made out of mustard greens, which remind me of home, instead of the usual basil. It's not the kind of pesto you'd eat raw on pasta, but it's wonderful in cooked dishes like this chicken.

SERVES 6

Pesto

> 2 cups chopped fresh mustard greens
> ¼ cup toasted pecans (see page 244)
> 1 tablespoon olive oil
> 1 garlic clove, minced or passed through a garlic press
> ¼ cup grated Parmesan cheese
> Salt

Combine the greens, pecans, and olive oil in a food processor and pulse until minced. (Alternatively, chop the nuts and mustard greens by hand, then combine them with the oil in a blender and blend until minced.) Add the garlic and pulse five or six more times. Add the Parmesan and salt to taste and pulse again. Place in a covered bowl and chill until ready to use, up to 3 days.

Chicken

> 6 boneless, skinless chicken breast halves (about 2¼ pounds)
> 2 tablespoons plus 2 teaspoons Faith's Special Seasoning (page 266) or
>   Cajun seasoning (see Sources, page 267)
> 1 teaspoon salt
> ⅓ cup plain yogurt
> 1 large egg
> 1 cup cornflakes
> 1 cup Grape-Nuts cereal
> 2 tablespoons olive oil

1. Preheat the oven to 375 degrees F. Rinse the chicken breasts and pat dry with paper towels. Pound the breasts flat to ¼ inch thick.
2. Season the chicken breasts with 1 tablespoon Faith's seasoning and the salt. In a shallow bowl, whisk together another tablespoon of Faith's seasoning with the yogurt and the egg. In another shallow bowl, combine the cornflakes and Grape-Nuts with the remaining 2 teaspoons of Faith's seasoning.
3. Coat the bottom of a baking pan with the olive oil. Spoon 2 tablespoons of mustard green pesto across the center of each breast, then fold the sides in, and roll it up. Dip each roll into the yogurt mixture, then coat with the cereal mixture. Place the breasts in the prepared baking dish seam side down.
4. Bake for 35 to 45 minutes, until the chicken juices run clear when pierced with a knife. Serve immediately.

Smoky Turkey Roast

In the South in the wintertime, or whenever the weather is cold and wet, hard-core grillers move the grill under their carports. But everyone else cooks indoors with liquid smoke. We often make "barbecue" in the oven using liquid smoke, to get that just-done, outside flavor.

During the holidays, this is the turkey we serve with cornbread dressing (see page 174) and mashed potatoes; At other times we just have it with rice. In fact, roasted turkey breast has become one of our favorite meals, especially since it's so healthy.

SERVES 6

> 4 tablespoons olive oil
> 2 celery stalks, chopped
> 1 large onion, chopped
> 2 garlic cloves, chopped
> 1 whole, bone-in turkey breast (6 to 7 pounds)
> 1½ tablespoons liquid smoke (see Sources, page 267)
> 1 tablespoon balsamic vinegar
> 1 tablespoon chopped fresh oregano,
>   or 1 teaspoon dried oregano
> Salt and black pepper
> 2 teaspoons Faith's Special Seasoning (page 266) or
>   Cajun seasoning (see Sources, page 267)
> 1 cup chicken broth, canned or homemade (page 72)
> 1 tablespoon all-purpose flour

1. Heat 1 tablespoon of the olive oil in a skillet. Add the celery, onion, and garlic and sauté over medium-high heat until the onions are slightly brown, about 10 minutes. Set aside.
2. Rinse the turkey breast and pat dry with paper towels. In a large bowl, whisk together the liquid smoke, the remaining 3 tablespoons olive oil, and the balsamic vinegar, oregano, and salt and pepper. Place the turkey breast in the bowl and rub the marinade all over it. Sprinkle with Faith's seasoning. Add the vegetables to the marinade, cover, and refrigerate for at least an hour, or overnight.

3. Remove the turkey from the refrigerator about 30 minutes before placing it in the oven. Preheat the oven to 350 degrees F.
4. Transfer the turkey, along with the marinade and vegetables, to a roasting pan. Roast for 20 minutes per pound (about 2 hours), rotating the turkey once or twice so it browns evenly. If the turkey gets as brown as you like it before the cooking time is up, cover it with a tent of foil and continue cooking. The turkey is done when the juices run clear when it is pricked.
5. Place the turkey on a platter and cover it loosely with foil. Transfer the contents of the roasting pan to a blender or food processor and blend or process until smooth. Transfer this mixture to a heavy skillet, bring it to a boil, and stir in the chicken broth. In a small dish, whisk together the flour and ½ cup water. Add this to the skillet and cook, stirring constantly, until thickened, about 5 minutes.
6. Carve the turkey and ladle gravy over it.

Mom's Dutch Oven Turkey Breast

This is a perfect everyday turkey recipe—not fancy, just good. It makes plenty, which is handy, since I loved the meals my mom made from the leftovers as much as I loved the original turkey breast!

Mom Says: Leftover turkey can be the base for several other meals. It's great for making Smoked Turkey Po' Boys (page 16) or pot pies (page 116), and then you can pick the rest of the meat from the bones and make turkey soup by simmering the bones for about 3 hours in a pot with some onion, salt, and pepper. Then just strain the stock and add more chopped vegetables and the picked turkey meat to the soup and simmer until the vegetables are done.

SERVES 6

1 whole, bone-in turkey breast (6 to 7 pounds)
7 tablespoons olive oil
2 tablespoons red wine vinegar
1 garlic clove, minced or passed through a garlic press
1½ teaspoons salt
½ teaspoon black pepper
1 tablespoon Faith's Special Seasoning (page 266) or
  Cajun seasoning (see Sources, page 267)
1 large onion, chopped
2 celery stalks, chopped
2 tablespoons all-purpose flour
1½ cups chicken broth, canned or homemade (page 72)

1. Rinse the turkey breast and pat dry with paper towels. Preheat the oven to 400 degrees F.
2. In a large bowl, whisk 6 tablespoons of the olive oil with the vinegar, garlic, salt, and pepper. Place the turkey in the bowl and rub it all over with the dressing. Sprinkle with Faith's seasoning.
3. Warm the remaining tablespoon of olive oil in a Dutch oven. Add the onion and celery and sauté over medium-high heat until softened, 5 to 7 minutes. Sprinkle 1 table-

spoon of the flour over the vegetables and stir it in thoroughly. Stir in ½ cup of the broth and turn off the heat.

4. Place the turkey, breast side down, on top of the vegetables in the Dutch oven. Pop on the lid and cook in the oven for 30 minutes, then turn the turkey breast side up. Return the pot to the oven, uncovered this time, reduce the heat to 350 degrees F, and bake for 45 minutes more, until the juices run clear when the breast is pierced with a small, sharp knife. Remove the pot from the oven, cover it, and let sit for 15 more minutes (the turkey will still be cooking in there). Transfer the turkey to a serving dish and cover it with foil.

5. Place the Dutch oven over medium-high heat and add the remaining cup broth. In a small bowl, whisk together ½ cup water and the remaining tablespoon of flour. Add this mixture to the pot and cook, stirring constantly, until thickened, about 5 minutes. Taste the gravy and add more salt and pepper if desired. Carve the turkey and serve with gravy.

Bacon-and-Sage-Wrapped
Turkey Breast

This recipe was one of those happy mistakes. I had bought a turkey breast to roast, and it wasn't until I started cooking that I realized, lo and behold, it was a boneless breast and would dry out in the oven. Since I happened to have some bacon around and some fresh sage, I wrapped the breast in the sage and then in the bacon, seared the whole thing, then finished it in the oven. It turned out so well that I thought it would be great instead of a whole turkey for Thanksgiving when there'd just be a handful around the table. You can also adapt the recipe for chicken breasts—just reduce the cooking time. Leftovers make terrific club sandwiches, since you've got both the turkey and bacon there already.

SERVES 6

> 1 whole boneless, skinless turkey breast (about 4 pounds), cut in half
> 2 tablespoons soy sauce
> 2 tablespoons Faith's Special Seasoning (page 266) or
>   Cajun seasoning (see Sources, page 267)
> 20 fresh sage leaves
> 1 pound sliced bacon
> 1 heaping tablespoon flour
> Salt and black pepper

1. Preheat the oven to 350 degrees F. Rinse the turkey breast and pat dry with paper towels.
2. Place the turkey breast halves in a large bowl and pour the soy sauce over them. Turn to coat well. Sprinkle on Faith's seasoning and rub in well. Arrange 10 sage leaves in a row on top of each piece of turkey. Wrap each half crosswise with bacon strips, covering the sage leaves. Starting from the top, secure the bacon ends to the turkey with toothpicks as each strip is wrapped around the turkey.
3. In a large, ovenproof pan or skillet over medium-high heat, sear the turkey for 5 minutes on each side, until the bacon starts to brown. Place the pan in the oven for 15 minutes. Turn the breasts and baste with the pan juices, then return to the oven for another 20 to 30 minutes, until the internal temperature reaches 160 degrees F.

Remove the turkey from the pan, cover with foil, and let it rest while you prepare the gravy.

4. Remove all but 2 tablespoons of the drippings from the pan and place it over medium heat. Add 1½ cups water to the pan drippings and boil for 5 minutes. In a small bowl, combine the flour with ¾ cup water and mix well, then stir this into the boiling mixture. Simmer and stir until the gravy is clear, about 5 minutes. Season with salt and pepper to taste.

5. Slice the turkey, drizzle the gravy over the slices, and serve.

Homey Pot Pies

Pot pies are a perfect way to use up leftovers. You can can make them with either chicken or turkey (or even sausage) and add different vegetables like potatoes, green beans, or bell peppers. Or leave the meat out altogether for a vegetarian meal (just make sure the filling adds up to 5 cups).

SERVES 6

Biscuit Topping

    2 cups self-rising flour (see Note, page 192)
    8 tablespoons (1 stick) unsalted butter, cut into small pieces
    ½ cup half-and-half

1. Combine the flour and butter in a food processor and pulse for a few seconds, until the mixture is in pea-sized pieces (alternatively, cut the flour and butter together in a bowl, using a pastry cutter or two knives). Add ¼ cup of the half-and-half and process for a few seconds more (or mix in with a fork), then add the remaining half-and-half and pulse or mix until a dough is formed. Do not overmix.
2. Turn the dough out onto a sheet of plastic wrap, pat into a circle, and refrigerate for 1 hour or up to 1 day.

Filling

    1½ cups chicken (or turkey) broth, canned or homemade (page 72)
    2 carrots, sliced
    3 tablespoons vegetable oil
    1 medium onion, chopped
    3 tablespoons all-purpose flour
    1 cup half-and-half
    3 cups chopped, cooked chicken or turkey meat (see Mom Says, page 102)
    1 cup frozen green peas
    Salt and black pepper
    2 tablespoons butter, melted

1. In a small saucepan bring the broth to a boil. Add the carrots, reduce the heat to medium, and simmer until just done, 4 to 5 minutes. Remove the carrots with a slotted spoon and set aside. Reserve the broth.

2. Heat the oil in a large saucepan over medium heat. Add the onion and cook until softened, 4 to 5 minutes. Stir in the flour and cook, stirring constantly, until nut-brown, about 3 minutes. Add the reserved broth, raise the heat, and bring to a boil. Cook, stirring, for a couple of minutes, until slightly thickened. Add the half-and-half and return the mixture to a boil, stirring. Reduce the heat to a gentle simmer and stir in the chicken or turkey, reserved carrots, peas, and salt and pepper to taste. Pour into a 9-by-9-inch pan.

3. Preheat the oven to 425 degrees F.

4. On a floured surface, roll out the biscuit dough to a ¾-inch thickness. Cut out biscuits, using a 3-inch round cookie cutter or the mouth of a glass, and place the biscuits on top of the chicken mixture. Bake for 20 minutes, then brush the tops of the biscuits with the melted butter and continue baking for another 10 minutes, until the biscuits are golden and the pie is bubbling. Serve hot.

Faith's Turkey and Veggie Meat Loaf with Fresh Salsa Gravy

My friend Patrick works in the fitness industry out here in L.A. He's also from the South. He and I are constantly searching for foods from home that we like and are healthful. When Patrick called and said, "Faith, you've got to taste the turkey meat loaf at Sports Club L.A. It tastes like food!" I said, "Oh, I'll believe that when I taste it." He was right about that meat loaf. I was amazed and inspired to develop my own recipe with vegetables instead of bread. But I added a fresh chunky salsa to make it zesty and spicy. That's how this red meat loaf evolved. It has become my house meat loaf, even though I was raised on my mom's brown beef meat loaf (see Tiny Meat Loaf for Two, page 142).

This recipe is great reheated. Instead of putting the whole thing back in the oven, I like to put a little olive oil in a skillet and sear leftover slices on both sides, then heat the sauce and put it over the top again. It feels like a different meal.

SERVES 4

Meat Loaf

> 2 tablespoons olive oil, plus additional for baking dish
> 1 small onion, finely chopped
> 3 garlic cloves, finely chopped
> 1 cup chunky salsa, preferably fresh (from the prepared foods
>   section of the grocery store)
> 1 small zucchini, grated
> 1 carrot, grated
> Salt and black pepper
> 1½ pounds ground turkey
> 1 tablespoon Faith's Special Seasoning (page 266) or
>   Cajun seasoning (see Sources, page 267)

1. Preheat the oven to 350 degrees F.
2. In a medium skillet over high heat, warm the 2 tablespoons olive oil. Add the onion and sauté for 5 to 7 minutes, until brown. Add the garlic and sauté for 30 seconds

more. Add the salsa and sauté for another 30 seconds. Stir in the zucchini and carrot and remove from the heat. Let cool a bit, then season with salt and pepper to taste.

3. Place the turkey in a large mixing bowl and sprinkle with Faith's seasoning. Add the vegetable mixture and work the seasoning and vegetables into the meat. Do not overmix.

4. Lightly coat a 9-by-12-inch baking dish with olive oil. Place the turkey mixture in the pan and shape it into a loaf using your cupped hands. At this point, the meat loaf can be covered and refrigerated for up to 8 hours. Bake for 15 minutes (20 minutes if the meat loaf was refrigerated), then add the salsa gravy (see below).

Salsa Gravy

2 tablespoons olive oil
½ small onion, chopped
2 tablespoons all-purpose flour
1 cup chicken broth, canned or homemade (page 72)
1 cup chunky salsa, preferably fresh (from the prepared foods section of the grocery store)
Salt and black pepper

1. As soon as you put the meat loaf in the oven, warm the oil in a small saucepan over medium heat. Add the onion and sauté until brown, 5 to 7 minutes. Stir in the flour and sauté for another minute. Add the chicken broth and stir until simmering. Add the salsa and bring to a simmer again. Cook, stirring, until thickened, 2 to 3 minutes more. Season to taste with salt and pepper.

2. Pour the gravy over the partially cooked meat loaf. Raise the oven temperature to 400 degrees F and bake until the top is browned and the inside of the meat loaf is cooked through and no longer pink (test it by making a small incision with a knife), about 30 minutes more.

Herb-and-Parmesan-Stuffed
Turkey Burgers on Toasted Garlic Buns

I started stuffing turkey burgers because I found them too dry when I did them on the grill and, when I mixed in seasonings, the flavor of the seasonings seemed to get lost. Burgers with flavorful ingredients stuffed in the center solve those problems and are a great surprise when you bite into them and discover an herb-and-cheese filling. They're also neater than regular burgers piled high with toppings. I love to serve these burgers with Pleasingly Purple Cabbage Salad (page 39). It's a pretty meal.

SERVES 4

Herb and Parmesan Filling
>   3 tablespoons olive oil
>   ¼ cup chopped onion
>   1 garlic clove, minced or passed through a garlic press
>   ¼ cup chopped fresh parsley
>   ¼ cup chopped fresh basil
>   ¼ cup grated Parmesan cheese

1. In a skillet over medium-high heat, warm 2 tablespoons of the oil. Add the onion and sauté until tender, about 3 minutes. Add the garlic and sauté for 2 minutes more. Let cool thoroughly.
2. In a food processor, combine the parsley, basil, and remaining tablespoon of oil and finely chop (or finely chop the herbs by hand and mix in the oil). Add the herbs to the onion and garlic mixture along with the Parmesan cheese and mix well. The filling can be made up to 2 days ahead, covered, and stored in the refrigerator.

Burgers
>   1 pound ground turkey
>   ½ cup plain dried bread crumbs
>   1 tablespoon Worcestershire sauce

1 tablespoon Faith's Special Seasoning (page 266) or
  Cajun seasoning (see Sources, page 267)
½ teaspoon salt
½ teaspoon black pepper
4 hamburger buns or rolls
Olive oil
1 garlic clove, cut in half
Regular or light mayonnaise
Dijon mustard
4 tomato slices, or 12 seedless cucumber slices
4 lettuce leaves, or 8 arugula leaves

1. In a bowl, combine the turkey, bread crumbs, Worcestershire sauce, Faith's seasoning, salt, and pepper and mix well.
2. Form the turkey mixture into 4 large patties, ½ inch thick. Make a depression in the
   middle of each. Place 1 tablespoon of stuffing in the center of each patty and fold the
   burger together and reshape into a stuffed patty about 1½ inches thick. Burger patties can be formed up to 1 day ahead, covered, and refrigerated. Or freeze them, well
   wrapped, for up to 1 month.
3. Preheat the stovetop grill if using. Grill the burgers for 5 to 7 minutes per side, until
   cooked through. Alternatively, heat 3 to 4 tablespoons olive oil in a skillet and cook
   the burgers for about 15 minutes, turning once during this time.
4. To serve, rub the cut sides of each bun all over with the garlic clove, then brush each
   with 1 tablespoon olive oil. Grill the buns (or toast in the skillet) until lightly browned
   and crispy. Spread one side of each grilled bun with mayonnaise and the other side
   with mustard. Place a burger on each bun, top with a slice of tomato or some cucumber slices and a lettuce leaf or two leaves of arugula, and serve immediately.

Curried Turkey, Brown Rice, and Veggie Hash

In this hash, the starch from the rice creates a little creaminess. My favorite rice to use here is brown basmati, but any leftover cooked rice works well—especially if it's a little under-cooked so it stands up to reheating. For me, spice is necessary, otherwise the hash is bland, but you can use jalapeños to taste. One of the most important ingredients in this recipe is the curry powder. Be sure yours is fresh, since it loses its zip after six months or so. To keep spices fresh longer, store them tightly capped, in a cool, dry place. I recommend taking an inventory of your seasonings every six months to a year and replacing anything that's been around so long it has no fragrance left.

SERVES 4

⅔ cup brown rice

2 tablespoons olive oil

1 medium onion, chopped

4 garlic cloves, minced or passed through a garlic press

1 celery stalk, chopped

1 tablespoon minced fresh ginger

1 pound ground turkey

1 tablespoon curry powder

1 teaspoon dry mustard powder

1 red bell pepper, chopped

1 teaspoon minced fresh or pickled jalapeño, or to taste, optional

2 medium yellow squash, cut into ¼-inch cubes

1 cup fresh or frozen petite green peas

1 cup chicken broth, canned or homemade (page 72)

3 ounces fresh spinach, chopped (about 3 cups)

⅓ cup finely chopped fresh cilantro

1½ teaspoons salt

½ teaspoon black pepper

1. Cook the rice according to the package directions.
2. Heat the olive oil in a wok or large skillet over medium heat. Add the onion and garlic and sauté until fragrant, about 1 minute. Add the celery and ginger and sauté for 1 minute more. Add the turkey, curry, and mustard powder and sauté until the turkey is no longer pink, about 6 minutes.
3. Stir in the bell pepper and jalapeño and sauté for 1 minute. Stir in the squash and sauté for 1 minute. Stir in the peas and sauté for 1 more minute. Add the chicken broth and bring to a boil, then stir in the cooked rice and let simmer for 2 to 3 minutes. The starch from the rice will give the mixture a creamy risotto consistency. Stir in the spinach, cilantro, salt, and pepper. Serve in large, shallow bowls.

CHAPTER 6

Meat

Golden Brown Beef Stew

Wintertime in Louisiana means freezing rain, branches breaking off under the weight of ice, and a wet cold that chills you to the bone. You really don't want to be out and about in it. It's messy and dangerous. My mom's beef stew was so nice and warming on days like that; it still is.

SERVES 4

2 pounds lean beef stew meat, rinsed, patted dry, and
    cut into 1½-inch pieces
Salt and pepper
2 tablespoons vegetable oil, plus more if needed
2 large onions
1 teaspoon minced garlic, optional
3 tablespoons all-purpose flour
3 cups water
3 celery stalks, cut into ½-inch pieces
4 potatoes, cut into chunks
4 medium carrots, sliced
1 (10-ounce) package frozen green peas

1. Preheat the oven to 350 degrees F.
2. Season the meat with salt and pepper. Heat the oil in a Dutch oven over medium-high heat, then add the meat. Turn the heat to high and sear the meat until it's browned on all sides, about 10 minutes. Transfer the meat to a plate.
3. Finely chop 1 of the onions. Add to the pot with the garlic and cook, stirring, until the onion browns, 5 to 10 minutes. Return the meat to the pot, sprinkle the flour into the pot and cook, stirring, until the flour browns, being careful not to scorch the mix. Add 1 tablespoon more oil if needed to prevent sticking.
4. Add the water a little at a time, stirring as the mixture comes to a boil. Boil for 10 minutes, then reduce the heat to a simmer. Cut the remaining onion into chunks and add to the pot with all the other vegetables; mix well to coat the the vegetables with the liquid. The liquid will not cover the vegetables.

5. Sprinkle lightly with salt and pepper, then place the pot, covered, in the oven and cook for 1 hour until the meat is tender. Do not peek. Remove from the oven and serve with cornbread or toasted French bread and salad.

From left: Me, my cousin Scott, and my sister, Devon, in one of our favorite places to sit: Grandpa Walker's lap.

Spicy Beef Stew with Vegetables and Tomatoes

This hearty stew is similar to Golden Brown Beef Stew (page 126), but it is red from tomatoes and spicy from jalapeño pepper. I like to add some chopped fresh herbs as a garnish, but you can skip that if you don't have any on hand. This is really a complete one-pot meal, though of course I would add a salad on the side.

SERVES 4

> 2 pounds lean beef stew meat, rinsed, patted dry, and
>   cut into 1½-inch cubes
> Salt and black pepper
> 2 tablespoons vegetable oil
> 1 large onion, chopped
> 2 medium carrots, sliced
> 2 celery stalks, chopped
> 1 green bell pepper, chopped
> 6 garlic cloves, chopped
> 1 jalapeño pepper, minced
> ¼ teaspoon crushed red pepper flakes
> 3 tablespoons all-purpose flour
> 1 (14-ounce) can diced tomatoes
> 4 small baking potatoes, cut into chunks
> Chopped fresh parsley or cilantro, optional

1. Season the meat with salt and pepper. Warm the oil in a Dutch oven over medium-high heat, then add the seasoned meat. Sear the meat until it's browned on all sides, about 10 minutes.
2. Transfer the meat to a plate and put the onion in the pot. Cook, stirring, until golden, about 10 minutes. Add the carrots, celery, bell pepper, garlic, jalapeño, and pepper flakes, and cook for another 5 minutes.
3. In a bowl, whisk together 1 cup water and the flour. Return the meat and its juices to the pot and add the water-flour mixture along with the tomatoes and potatoes. Top

up the stew with water until the liquid reaches approximately two-thirds to the level of the meat and vegetables (it should not cover the ingredients in the pot). Partially cover the pot and simmer until the meat is tender, about 1 hour and 30 minutes, stirring occasionally.

4. Serve immediately, garnished with cilantro or parsley if desired, or let cool, then cover and refrigerate overnight. Reheat before serving.

Mom's Smoky Beef Brisket

The secret to this juicy, tender brisket is marinating the meat overnight in a dark brown flavoring called liquid smoke (you can buy it at the supermarket or mail order it). It gives it a barbecued flavor without your having to set up the grill. The slower you cook this brisket, the more tender it becomes, which means more flavor. It's really good served with Oven-Baked Sour Cream and Cheese Mashed Potatoes (page 170) and, of course, a green salad.

✣ *Mom Says:* Leftovers are a great addition to soups, especially my beef vegetable soup recipe on page 64.

SERVES 12

> 1 brisket (6 to 7 pounds), trimmed, rinsed, and patted dry
> ¼ cup Worcestershire sauce
> ¼ cup packed dark brown sugar
> 2 tablespoons liquid smoke (see Sources, page 267)
> 2 tablespoons balsamic vinegar
> 2 garlic cloves, minced or passed through a garlic press
> Salt and black pepper
> 1 large onion, minced

1. Place the brisket in a Dutch oven or heavy roasting pan. Mix together the Worcestershire sauce, brown sugar, liquid smoke, vinegar, and garlic. Pour the mixture over the brisket and rub it all over. Sprinkle all sides of the meat with salt and black pepper.
2. Lift the brisket and spread the onion underneath to create a layer between the meat and the bottom of the pan. The onion will be hardly visible when the cooking is finished. Cover the pan and refrigerate it overnight so the smoky seasoning fully penetrates the meat.
3. Preheat the oven to 450 degrees F.
4. Place the brisket, still covered, in the oven for 15 minutes to heat up the roasting pan quickly, then reduce the heat to 300 degrees F and roast the meat for 2¼ to 3 hours. Check for tenderness by piercing the thickest part of the brisket with a fork—if the meat slips off easily, it's done.

5. Allow the meat to sit in its juices until near serving time (at least 20 minutes and up to 4 hours). Any excess fat can be skimmed from the juices at this time. If you are refrigerating any leftovers, the fat will congeal and it is easy to remove almost all of it. Or you can make this a day ahead, cool, cover and refrigerate it, then remove the fat, reheat, and serve warm or at room temperature.

My husband, Campion, and me, making gravy for
Thanksgiving dinner in our Los Angeles home.

Smothered Steak with Onion Gravy

This was one of the recipes my mom would make on Sundays. She would get everything ready before church, then quickly finish it when we got home, so there would be a hot, hardy meal right away. It's also perfect to make after work on a weeknight, since it cooks so fast. Everyone will love the rich, oniony flavor of the gravy.

Mom Says: This gravy is what is known as "flour gravy" in the South, and it was a staple in the Southern diet. During the Depression many people survived on flour gravy and biscuits and whatever they could hunt: ducks, quail, deer, rabbits, and squirrels.

Flour gravy was always a rich brown at our house, and my mother's gravy always had a smooth consistency. It was never too thick or difficult to spoon. She was so good at making gravy that she left all the browned pieces in the skillet after pouring out most of the oil and just added the flour. It made the gravy better. I have trouble with the bits getting too brown and starting to burn before the flour browns, so I add water to the pan to loosen them, then I pour that water into a cup and wipe out the pan before frying the flour. When you pour the water back into the pan you're returning all the flavor from those browned bits.

SERVES 4

> 1½ to 2 pounds tenderized round or cube steak,
>   cut into 4 serving-sized portions, rinsed and patted dry
> Salt and black pepper
> ¾ cup all-purpose flour
> ½ cup vegetable oil
> 1 large sweet onion, thinly sliced

1. Sprinkle each side of the steaks very lightly with salt and pepper. Place the flour in a plastic container with a lid. Add two pieces of steak to the flour, seal the lid, and shake to coat the steak with flour. Transfer the meat to a plate and repeat the process

until all the steaks are generously floured. Alternatively, spread the flour out on a plate and dredge the steaks on both sides, shaking off any excess. Reserve the flour.

2. In a skillet, heat the oil until a pinch of flour sizzles when sprinkled in. Use tongs to place two of the steaks in the hot oil and fry them until the undersides are brown, 5 to 7 minutes. Turn and brown the other sides, 2 to 3 minutes more. Remove the steaks and drain them on a paper towel–lined plate. Repeat with the remaining steaks. Turn off the heat.

3. Using protective mitts, pour the oil into a glass measuring cup. Add 2 cups water to the pan and stir, loosening the browned bits sticking to the bottom of the skillet. Transfer the liquid from the skillet to a second measuring cup and reserve. Use paper towels to dry the pan before measuring ¼ cup of the oil back into the pan.

4. Add ⅓ cup of the reserved flour to the skillet. On medium-high heat, cook the oil and flour, stirring constantly, to make a rich brown roux (it will look like coffee with cream), about 10 minutes. Return the 2 cups reserved liquid to the pan and stir as the gravy simmers and thickens. Reduce the heat to medium to prevent boiling over. Add 1 teaspoon salt and ¼ teaspoon black pepper and cook for 5 to 6 minutes longer.

5. Place half of the sliced onion in the gravy, return the fried steak to the skillet, place the remaining onion slices on top, pop on the cover, and simmer the meat over low heat until the steaks are tender, 20 to 30 minutes. Serve hot, with the gravy.

Juicy Beef Pot Roast

This family beef roast is cooked the same way as the Old-Fashioned Oven Pork Pot Roast (page 136), but they have completely different flavors. The pork is a little richer and spicier while the beef is mellower. I love them both, though the beef has one big advantage over the pork—leftovers are perfect for making Rest of the Pot Roast Po' Boys (page 12) the next day. When you start slicing this roast up, some little bits come off the sides. That's called the debris. You can take all those little bits and put them in your gravy, but I just eat them on the side or pile them onto my po' boy. They're the best part!

SERVES 8

> 1 lean beef roast (4 to 5 pounds), trimmed, rinsed, and patted dry
> Salt and black pepper
> Faith's Special Seasoning (page 266) or
>   Cajun seasoning (see Sources, page 267)
> 3 garlic cloves, halved and sliced lengthwise into spears
> 2 tablespoons vegetable oil
> 1 large onion, chopped
> 1 cup water
> 2 heaping tablespoons all-purpose flour

1. Preheat the oven to 350 degrees F.
2. Lightly season the roast on all sides with salt, pepper, and Faith's seasoning. Pierce the roast all over with a small paring knife and press the garlic spears into the holes so that they are no longer visible.
3. In a Dutch oven or heavy roasting pan over high heat, warm the oil. Carefully place the roast in the pan and cook, turning it, until it is really brown on all sides, 10 to 15 minutes. Transfer the roast to a plate and set it aside.
4. Reduce the heat to medium-high. Add the onion to the pan and cook, stirring, until golden, about 7 minutes. Add the water and let it come to a boil, stirring and scraping any browned bits from the bottom of the pan. Push the onion toward the center of the pan and lay the beef on top.
5. Cover the pan (with foil if you are using a roasting pan) and place it in the oven for 40 minutes. Turn the roast over, adding additional water if necessary so the bottom

of the pan has an inch of liquid. Cover the pan again and cook until the roast is tender and the internal temperature of the meat reaches 140 degrees F, another 25 to 35 minutes.

6. Place the pan on the stovetop and transfer the roast to a carving board. Cover the meat with foil to keep it warm.

7. For the gravy, in a small bowl, stir the flour into 1 cup water. Strain this mixture into the remaining juices in the pan. Bring the liquid to a boil over medium heat, stirring and scraping the bottom of the pan. Reduce the heat and simmer for 15 minutes, stirring frequently. Season with salt and pepper.

8. Slice the roast and serve with plenty of the gravy. Save the leftovers for sandwiches.

Old-Fashioned Oven Pork Pot Roast

People in the South traditionally eat a lot of pork all year long, but when New Year's rolls around, it's practically mandatory, especially in our family. They say that eating pork on New Year's brings you good health for the next year. When I was growing up, the centerpiece of our family's New Year's dinner was always this old-fashioned pork roast. We served it with black-eyed peas and Grandpa Walker's Favorite Crunchy Southern Slaw (page 38), since eating cabbage on New Year's was supposed to bring you money, and having black-eyed peas meant you'd never go hungry. Of course it's also a delicious, homey roast for any time of year—we always serve it with rice or mashed potatoes.

SERVES 8

> 1 lean pork roast (4 to 5 pounds), trimmed, rinsed, and patted dry
> Salt and black pepper
> Faith's Special Seasoning (page 266) or
> Cajun seasoning (see Sources, page 267)
> 4 garlic cloves, halved and sliced lengthwise into spears, optional
> 2 tablespoons vegetable oil
> 1 large onion, chopped
> 2 cups water
> 2 heaping tablespoons all-purpose flour

1. Preheat the oven to 350 degrees F.
2. Lightly season the roast on all sides with salt, pepper, and Faith's seasoning. Pierce the roast all over with a small paring knife and press the garlic spears into the holes so that they are no longer visible.
3. In a Dutch oven or heavy roasting pan over high heat, warm the oil. Carefully place the roast in the pan and cook, turning it, until it is really brown on all sides, about 10 minutes. Transfer the roast to a plate and set it aside.
4. Reduce the heat to medium-high. Put the onion in the pan and cook, stirring, until golden, about 7 minutes. Add 1 cup of the water and let it come to a boil, stirring and

scraping any browned bits from the bottom of the pan. Push the onion toward the center of the pan and lay the pork roast on top.

5. Cover the pan (with foil if you are using a roasting pan) and place it in the oven for 45 minutes. Turn the roast over, adding additional water if necessary so the bottom of the pan has an inch of liquid. Cover the pan again and cook until the internal temperature of the roast reaches 160 degrees F, about another 45 minutes.

6. Place the pan on the stovetop and transfer the roast to a carving board. Cover the meat with foil to keep warm.

7. For the gravy, in a small bowl, stir the flour into the remaining cup of water. Strain this mixture into the remaining juices in the pan. Bring the liquid to a boil over medium heat, stirring and scraping the bottom of the pan. Reduce the heat and simmer for 15 minutes, stirring frequently. Season with salt and pepper if needed.

8. Slice the roast into ½-inch-thick slices and serve it with the gravy.

Citrus-Roasted Pork Loin

These days, I am choosy about the cuts of pork I cook. Usually I look for something lean, like pork tenderloin. But when I was very young, and especially when my parents were growing up, my family ate every cut of pork. My grandpa Walker used to say, "We used every part of the pig except for the squeal." They cooked the feet, the snout, the head (which got made into hogshead cheese), the chitlins, and the skin for cracklings, and they rendered the pork fat to cook with. Back when most people didn't have electric refrigerators, pork was important because you could smoke it and it would last and last. My grandparents raised pigs, and their pork had amazing flavor and was always very tender. Even the leanest cuts, like the loin, were nice and juicy.

This is my version of a pork loin roast. It's one of those recipes I'll make when I'm homesick, since pork roast always reminds me of the holidays at my grandma Cora's house. Over the years, I've changed her recipe to suit my own tastes, making it fresher and brighter-tasting by marinating the meat in orange and lemon juices, cumin, and oregano. It's a great dish for a small dinner party—one pork loin is perfect for six. Or you can double the recipe. Leftover pork is terrific in sandwiches, and the lemony gravy is fantastic over rice or potatoes the next day. Or use the pork and gravy in Black-Eyed Pea Soup with Sausage and Mustard Greens (page 61).

SERVES 6

1 pork loin roast (2½ to 3 pounds), trimmed, rinsed, and patted dry

½ cup orange juice, preferably freshly squeezed

¾ cup freshly squeezed lemon juice

10 garlic cloves, minced or passed through a garlic press

2 tablespoons chopped fresh oregano, or 2 teaspoons
    dried and crumbled oregano

1 teaspoon ground cumin

2 teaspoons salt

1 teaspoon black pepper

2 tablespoons olive oil

1 large onion, chopped

2 cups chicken broth, canned or homemade (page 72)

2 tablespoons all-purpose flour

1. Place the pork in a large nonreactive baking dish (or use a big plastic container like I do). Whisk together the orange and lemon juices, garlic, oregano, cumin, salt, and pepper. Score the roast in a crosshatch pattern across the top and pour on the marinade, making sure to rub the garlic into the slits on top. Cover the pork and let it marinate in the refrigerator for at least 12 hours, turning it once after about 6 hours.
2. Preheat the oven to 350 degrees F.
3. Take the roast out of the marinade, pat it dry, and season it with a bit of salt and pepper if desired. Warm the olive oil in a Dutch oven or heavy roasting pan. Sear the roast over medium-high heat until all sides are brown, about 15 minutes. Transfer the roast to a plate.
4. Add the onion to the pot and cook, stirring, until brown, 3 to 5 minutes.
5. Return the roast to the pot, add the marinade and chicken broth, and pop on the lid (or cover with foil if you are using a roasting pan). Place the pan in the oven and roast the pork for 30 minutes. Turn the roast over and continue cooking, covered, for 30 to 45 minutes more, until the interior temperature reaches 160 degrees F. Remove the roast from the pan and cover it loosely with foil until ready to serve.
6. For the gravy, place the pan on the stove and skim any excess fat. If the liquid is too salty, add a piece of potato and it will soak up excess salt (a tip from Grandma Bernice—just remember to discard the potato before serving). In a small bowl, stir the flour into ½ cup water. Strain this mixture into the remaining juices in the pan. Bring the liquid to a boil over medium heat, stirring and scraping the bottom of the pan. Reduce the heat and simmer for 5 minutes, stirring frequently.
7. Cut the pork into ½-inch slices and serve it with the gravy over rice.

Lunch with Grandpa Walker: or, the Nap

My grandma Cora would have lunch on the table by 11:30 A.M. every day. As soon as she set it out, she'd start calling my grandpa. He liked to come inside during the heat of the day to have his lunch. And he liked eating pretty much everything. He used to say to my mom, "Trisher, this is goood. This is goood." And, whenever he finished eating lunch, he'd say "Man that was goood." Then he'd just lie right down on the floor next to the dining room table and take a little nap. When he was all done napping, he'd sit right up, and say, "Cora, get me some of that Speederinktom"—his old dark-roast drip coffee, made in an old-fashioned coffeepot on the stovetop. A cup of that coffee perked him right back up, and back out to the fields he went.

"Hammy" Cabbage, Peas, and Carrots Stew

The good thing about ham is that it's got an intense flavor, so you don't need a lot of it to make this vegetable-based dish really flavorful. Serve with cornbread (page 198) to sop up the spicy, salty juices.

↭ *Mom Says:* This recipe was created to use leftover ham from Christmas dinner, since these days that is the only time that we buy a cured ham. If you don't have ham around, you can use smoked turkey sausage instead.

SERVES 4

2 tablespoons olive oil
2 cups ham or turkey sausage cut into 1-inch chunks
1 (14-ounce) can diced tomatoes
$\frac{1}{2}$ teaspoon hot sauce, or to taste
$\frac{1}{2}$ small head green cabbage, cut into small chunks (about 6 cups)
1 (16-ounce) package frozen peas and carrots
Salt and black pepper

1. Warm the olive oil in a Dutch oven or heavy pan over medium-high heat. Add the ham chunks and sauté until slightly browned on all sides, about 5 minutes. Add 1$\frac{1}{4}$ cups water and bring to a boil; let simmer for 10 minutes. Add the tomatoes and hot sauce and continue to cook for 5 minutes longer. The stew can be made ahead up to this point and cooled, covered, and refrigerated for up to 3 days.
2. Add the cabbage and peas and carrots, reduce the heat to medium-low, cover, and cook for 10 minutes. Remove the lid and stir well. Cover the stew and cook it for 5 or 10 minutes longer; the vegetables should be crisp, bright, and spicy. Season to taste with salt and pepper. Serve immediately or let cool, then cover and refrigerate overnight. Reheat before serving.

Tiny Meat Loaf for Two

When the ground beef came out of the freezer the night before, we knew my mom was about to make something easy, quick, and really good. In the mornings she would have her coffee, make up the meat loaf, then go to work. When she got home she'd just stick the meat loaf in the oven to cook while she made the rest of our meal. Typically she'd serve it with a vegetable and rice, or if there were a few leftover potatoes, she'd mash them. This tiny meat loaf is the smaller version she now makes when it's just she and my dad. It makes just enough for supper with a small amount left over for a sandwich the next day.

✢ **Mom Says:** You can use ground turkey instead of beef for this meat loaf if you prefer. And of course you can double the recipe and make two meat loaves to feed four people.

SERVES 2

> 1 large onion, thinly sliced
> ½ teaspoon brown sugar
> ½ teaspoon salt
> 4 tablespoons vegetable oil
> 3 tablespoons all-purpose flour
> 3 cups water
> ½ small onion, chopped
> ½ small baking potato, cubed
> ¼ green bell pepper, chopped
> 1 pound lean ground beef
> 1 teaspoon Faith's Special Seasoning (page 266) or
>   Cajun seasoning (see Sources, page 267)
> ½ teaspoon pepper

1. Preheat the oven to 400 degrees F.
2. In a Dutch oven or heavy roasting pan over medium-high heat, put the sliced onion, brown sugar, and salt and brown for 5 minutes. Add 2 tablespoons of the oil, reduce the heat to medium, and sauté for 10 to 15 minutes, until the onion is dark brown. Sprinkle 2 tablespoons of the flour over the onions and add the remaining 2 table-

spoons oil, stirring until the flour browns, about 10 minutes. Add 2 cups of the water, bring to a boil, and let cook until the liquid reduces by half to make an onion gravy.

3. Place the chopped onion, potato, and bell pepper in a food processor or on a chopping board and mince. In a bowl, combine the minced vegetables with the ground meat, Faith's seasoning, salt, and pepper. When these ingredients are well combined, form the mixture into a 5-by-3-inch loaf.

4. Place the meat loaf in the onion gravy and spoon the gravy over the top of the meat loaf. Cover and turn up the heat to bring everything to a sizzle (this takes only 1 minute or so).

5. Turn off the heat and transfer the pan to the oven. Reduce the heat to 350 degrees F and bake for 30 minutes. Check for doneness by cutting the loaf in half and spreading it apart. If the loaf is still pink in the center, replace the lid and return it to the oven for about 10 minutes more. Transfer the loaf to a serving platter and cover it with a tent of foil to keep it warm.

6. Mix the remaining 1 tablespoon flour in the remaining 1 cup water and stir into the gravy. Simmer for 10 minutes, or until the gravy is reduced to the desired consistency. Serve the meat loaf with the gravy on the side.

"Student Union" Burger on the Griddle

When she was in college, my mother worked part time at the Student Union building, and her boss, Mr. Johnson, taught her how to make the perfect burger. The trick is in the timing, getting the burgers and buns done at the right time and having all your fixings ready so you can slap the mayo, mustard, tomatoes, and lettuce on just before serving. The result is a burger that's crispy and warm without a soggy bun. The burgers are great with cheese, too.

⚜ *Mom Says:* These burgers have a little bread mixed right in with the meat, which helps keep them moist. If the crust on my white bread doesn't look like it will mix up well, then I usually take it off. Mr. Johnson, who taught me this recipe, would just scoop out the inside of the hamburger buns, and you can do that, too. At the Student Union, we'd freeze the shaped patties before we cooked them. They can be frozen, well wrapped, for up to a month. They'll defrost in 30 minutes or so. The trick here is that the bun goes face down on the griddle (you can use a skillet, too) like the bread for a po' boy, so you're actually toasting it in the fat from the meat. Then you just put your mayo on one side, mustard on the other side, and layer the burger, a slice of sweet onion, slice of tomato, and a leaf of lettuce in between the pieces of bread. You can always melt a slice of cheese on the burger just before it's done if you prefer a cheeseburger. Either way, that is the typical old-fashioned Southern hamburger. Burger on a griddle. We called it a grill, but people might think you're talking about an outdoor grill.

SERVES 4

> 1 slice white bread or ½ hamburger bun
> ½ teaspoon salt, or to taste
> ¼ teaspoon black pepper, or to taste
> 1 pound ground beef
> 2 tablespoons butter, melted
> 4 hamburger buns or rolls
> Light or regular mayonnaise
> Dijon mustard

4 slices sweet white onion
4 slices tomato
4 lettuce leaves

1. In a bowl, combine the bread with 2 tablespoons water and mix until soggy and soft. Add the salt and pepper to taste and stir in the meat. Form the mixture into 4 large patties 1 to 1½ inches thick. The burgers can be made a day ahead, covered, and refrigerated, or well wrapped individually and frozen for up to 1 month. Defrost before proceeding.
2. Warm a griddle or skillet on the stovetop over medium-high heat, then place the patties on it and cook them for 3 to 5 minutes. Flip the patties and cook them for 3 to 5 minutes more, until done to taste (to check for doneness, use a thin paring knife to cut a little into the center of a burger). Transfer the burgers to a plate and cover them with foil to keep them warm while you toast the buns.
3. Brush melted butter on both sides of each bun, then toast the buns on the hot griddle for 2 to 3 minutes, until browned.
4. Spread mayonnaise on one side of each toasted bun and mustard on the other. Top with a burger, a slice of sweet onion, a slice of tomato, and a lettuce leaf, and serve.

Mom's Stuffed Cabbage Rolls with Sweet Cabbage Sauté

My mom based this sweet cabbage sauté on my grandma Cora's skillet-caramelized cabbage. The cabbage browns a little on the bottom and gets sweet and tender. As my mom and I were working on this recipe, I started stirring the cabbage and she said, "No, no, don't stir it! You have to wait until it just starts to burn on the bottom, then flip it over." Stirring keeps it from getting nice and brown, which is the key to the amazing flavor.

⤜ **Mom Says:** Faith wanted to include my sweet-and-sour cabbage rolls in the book because she loved them when she was a little girl. But I had not made them in years and had no recipe written down, so we went into the kitchen and made this new version. Faith came up with the sauce and gave suggestions for the filling. A true team effort!

SERVES 4

Sauce

    2 tablespoons olive oil
    2 garlic cloves, minced or passed through a garlic press
    1 (29-ounce) can tomato puree
    ½ medium tomato, diced
    1½ tablespoons sugar
    1 tablespoon chopped fresh basil, or 1 teaspoon dried basil
    1 tablespoon chopped fresh oregano, or 1 teaspoon dried oregano
    1 teaspoon salt
    ½ teaspoon hot sauce, or to taste

In a skillet over medium-high heat, warm the oil. Add the garlic and sauté for 1 to 2 minutes, until fragrant. Add the remaining ingredients and simmer until slightly thickened, about 10 minutes. The sauce can be prepared up to 3 days ahead and cooled, covered, and refrigerated.

Cabbage Rolls

    1 tablespoon vegetable oil

    1 small onion, finely chopped

    ½ red bell pepper, finely chopped

    1 celery stalk, finely chopped

    2 garlic cloves, minced or passed through a garlic press

    1 pound ground beef or turkey

    2 cups frozen corn kernels

    1 cup cooked white or brown rice (from about ½ cup raw rice
       prepared according to package directions)

    ½ medium tomato, diced

    1 teaspoon hot sauce

    2 teaspoons Faith's Special Seasoning (page 266) or
       Cajun seasoning (see Sources, page 267)

    1 large head green cabbage

    1 teaspoon salt, if blanching the cabbage

    ½ cup grated Parmesan cheese

1. In a large skillet over medium-high heat, warm the oil. Add the onion, bell pepper, celery, and garlic and sauté for 5 minutes, until the vegetables wilt. Add the ground meat, breaking it apart as it sautés, and cook until it's no longer pink, about 5 minutes. Add the corn, rice, tomato, hot sauce, and Faith's seasoning and cook for 10 to 12 minutes, until most of the liquid has cooked away. Turn off the heat and cover the pan while you prepare the cabbage. The filling can be made 1 day ahead and cooled, covered, and refrigerated. Let it come to room temperature before proceeding.

2. Preheat the oven to 375 degrees F.

3. Remove the large loose green outer leaves from the cabbage and discard them. Wash the cabbage with cool water. Use a paring knife to remove the core of the cabbage without damaging any leaves. Add 2 inches of water to a large stockpot with a colander insert or steamer rack placed on the bottom. Place the cabbage, cut side down, on the rack and bring the water to a boil over high heat. Cover the pot when the water boils and steam the cabbage for 5 to 10 minutes, until tender. Transfer the cabbage to a plate and let it cool slightly. Carefully remove eight to nine large, flat leaves, one at a time, making sure not to tear them. When the leaves become difficult to remove, return the cabbage to the steamer and steam for about 5 minutes more, then continue removing leaves until you have about eight leaves. Save the remaining part of the cabbage head. (Alternatively, you can blanch the head of cabbage in boiling, well-salted

water for 30 seconds. As you are peeling off the leaves and they become difficult to remove, blanch again for 30 seconds and continue until you have about eight leaves.)

4. To make the rolls, use ¼ to ½ cup filling per leaf, depending on the size of the leaf. Place the filling near the stem and spread it sausage-like across each leaf. Start at the stem end and fold the cabbage over the meat once, then fold each side over to hold in the meat. Roll tightly to the outer end of the leaf. The rolls should be about 6 inches long. Place the rolls, seam side down, in an oblong baking dish. Cover and refrigerate overnight if desired.

5. Pour the sauce over and around the cabbage rolls. Sprinkle the tops with Parmesan cheese, and bake until the sauce is bubbling, about 30 minutes (35 to 40 minutes if the rolls were refrigerated).

Sweet Cabbage Sauté
> 1 tablespoon sugar
> 1 teaspoon salt
> 2 tablespoons olive oil
> 1 tablespoon red wine vinegar

1. Quarter, core, and shred the remaining inner cabbage leaves and place in a bowl. Add the sugar and salt and mix to coat the cabbage.

2. In a skillet over medium-high heat, warm the oil. Add the cabbage and let it cook, without stirring, until it is lightly brown on the bottom, about 6 minutes. Use a wide, flat spatula to turn the cabbage over (it's okay if it breaks apart, just pat it back together) and continue to cook until the other side is brown, about 5 minutes longer. Stir in the vinegar and remove the pan from the heat. Serve alongside the cabbage rolls and sauce.

CHAPTER 7

Side Dishes

Southern-Style Mustard Greens

I have always loved the tangy flavor of mustard greens. We grew them in the garden, and when we were kids, my sister and I would tear the leaves (which were bigger than our heads!) from the plants and run into the kitchen with them for my mom to cook. To make them, my mother would first slowly cook a piece of salt pork or bacon to render the flavorful fat, then cut the greens up right over the pot. She'd pile them into a stack, roll them up, and shred them. She'd always fill up a big huge pot, then fill it half full with water and cook the greens down until they were nice and tender.

We used to eat our greens with hot pepper sauce and fresh cornbread. The smoky bacon-flavored broth was good, too; we'd drink it like soup. I didn't realize how nutritious the pot liquor was for you at the time—I just knew I loved it. Now, I also know it contains a lot of the vitamins and nutrients from the greens. If you can't get good, fresh mustard greens, substitute frozen, which are already cut up for you and will cook more quickly, too.

SERVES 4

3 slices bacon or turkey bacon, or 1 ham hock
2 large bunches mustard greens, stalks removed, washed well, and
    chopped (about 12 cups), or 3 (10-ounce) packages frozen
    mustard greens, thawed
1 teaspoon salt, or to taste
Hot sauce

1. Put the bacon or ham in a heavy-bottomed pot with a lid and fry slowly over medium heat until golden brown, about 5 minutes. Pour off the fat if desired, add 4 cups water to the pot, and bring to a simmer.
2. Add the greens a handful at a time. They will wilt immediately, making room for more. Push the greens down into the liquid with a wooden spoon when all the leaves have been added. Cook at a rolling boil for about 5 minutes, reduce the heat to medium, and cover. Cook for 5 minutes, remove the lid, and stir in the salt. Replace the lid, reduce the heat to low, and cook slowly until the greens lose their bright color and are as tender as you like, 10 to 40 minutes (frozen greens will cook quicker than fresh).
3. Taste the greens and add a little more salt if needed. Serve hot with the pan liquid and pass the hot sauce on the side. The remaining liquid can be added to a vegetable soup.

Faith's Double "S" Mustard Greens

Although I love the old-fashioned way of cooking mustard greens, I also sometimes want to make them without the pork, so I came up with this recipe. The Double "S" stands for simmered and sautéed, which is how the greens are cooked. Since I remove all the stems and chop them small, they cook pretty quickly. You can use frozen greens, too—they work really well, and they're already chopped for you.

A lot of people I know, including myself, like their vegetables and greens cooked until just done. Others say that greens aren't greens unless they're completely tender and almost melting. Here I give an option for each camp. Either way, these are great with pepper sauce—a spicy sauce made from vinegar and hot peppers.

SERVES 4

Salt
1 tablespoon olive oil
2 slices turkey bacon, cut into ½-inch pieces
2 large bunches mustard greens, stalks removed, washed well,
    and chopped (about 12 cups)
Pepper sauce, optional

1. Bring a pot of well-salted water to a rolling boil. Meanwhile, in a heavy skillet with a lid, warm the olive oil over medium heat. Add the turkey bacon and fry over medium heat until golden brown, about 3 minutes.
2. When the water boils, add the greens and boil for 2 minutes. Reserve ½ cup of the cooking liquid and then drain the greens.
3. Transfer the greens, along with 2 tablespoons of the reserved cooking liquid, to the pot with the bacon. Cover and cook over medium heat for 15 minutes, adding more of the reserved cooking liquid if needed. Taste the greens and add salt if you like.
4. If you prefer your greens even more tender, reduce the heat to low and simmer, covered, for another 30 minutes. Serve hot, with the pepper sauce or without.

All-Vegetable Meals

Every summer when my sister and I were young, we would help harvest the corn at Grandpa Walker's farm. At the end of the summer, the height of the season for produce, the farm and garden were full of ripe vegetables—mustard greens, turnip greens, squash, peas, okra, corn, tomatoes, and cabbage. Given the abundance, sometimes fresh vegetables were practically all we ate for days at a time. We had to eat fast to keep up with them! To this day, the memories of those "all-vegetable meals" make me hungry and happy. It was and still is one of my favorite ways to eat. This didn't mean the meals were vegetarian, though. There was always a little bit of bacon in the beans, ham in the greens, or pork sausage with the cabbage. But those farm-fresh vegetables had the spotlight.

I remember Grandma Cora shaving the kernels off the corncobs to make creamed corn. She would cook big pans of it just with salt and pepper. The flavor was so sweet and good it didn't need anything else. And then there was plenty of crispy fried okra, sweet juicy tomatoes, simmering greens, and (my favorites) purple hull peas, which we would eat with a piece of cornbread or a biscuit to soak up all the juices.

Desserts were also from the garden, made from the peaches or figs from my grandma's trees. And my grandpa sometimes grew sugar cane to make cane syrup with, so we could pour that on our biscuits as a sweet treat. It is a little like molasses. I still love it. You can order it by mail (see Sources, page 267).

Those fresh, healthy summertime meals are something that people must do anywhere they grow a lot of their own fruits and vegetables. It's not what you think of when you think of Southern food, but it was an important part of how we ate. After we ate our fill, we would put up vegetables to make soups and stews the rest of the year, and we would make fig preserves (page 265) to use in cakes. But when everything was as fresh as possible, we ate as much of it as we could, and the flavors were so fantastic that it was all you needed for an incredibly satisfying meal.

Stewed Okra and Tomatoes

My grandma Bernice loved stewed okra and tomatoes, always taken straight from the brimming garden. In the height of the summer, all she needed to add was some salt and pepper, and there was an instant vegetable side dish. She made lots and froze some in plastic bags to use year-round, either alone or in soups and stews.

I think a lot of people shy away from okra because they think it's slimy. But if you cook it right, it's delicious. Since I like my food on the spicy side, I've included a variation that uses jalapeño and garlic. Both versions are great served hot with homemade cornbread (page 198).

SERVES 4

> 1 slice bacon (or 2 teaspoons olive oil)
> 1 small onion, chopped
> 10 medium pods fresh okra, trimmed and sliced into ½-inch-thick rounds
> (about 2½ cups), or 1 (10-ounce) package frozen sliced okra
> 3 to 4 medium tomatoes, cored and chopped
> ½ teaspoon salt

1. Put the bacon (or turkey bacon and oil) in a medium saucepan with a lid and fry slowly over medium heat until golden brown, about 5 minutes. Remove the bacon to a paper towel–lined plate and crumble when cool. (If not using bacon, warm the olive oil in the saucepan over medium heat.)
2. Add the onion and sauté for 2 minutes. Add the okra, tomatoes, crumbled bacon, and salt and stir to combine.
3. Cover and cook over low heat until the okra is crisp-tender, not falling apart, about 15 minutes. Serve immediately, or let cool, then cover and refrigerate for up to 2 days. Reheat before serving.

Hot and Spicy Variation

Add 1 jalapeño pepper, seeded and chopped, and 2 garlic cloves, minced or passed through a garlic press, along with the onion.

Crispy Traditional
Southern-Fried Okra

My grandma Cora was big on fried okra; a lot of Southerners are. In most recipes, people make up a thick cornmeal batter, so they're kind of like okra fritters—more batter than okra. At our house we just lightly dusted the pods with cornmeal and salt, then fried them up. They were crunchy and salty and completely addictive.

We'd have our fried okra in the height of summer, as part of an all-vegetable meal with corn, peas, butter beans, mustard greens, and of course, cornbread to sop up the juices. My mother served her greens on the side, in bowls, so the juice wouldn't get into our fried okra and turn it soggy.

SERVES 4

> **Vegetable oil, for frying**
> **20 pods fresh okra, trimmed and sliced into**
> **½-inch-thick rounds (about 5 cups)**
> **1 cup cornmeal**
> **½ teaspoon salt**

1. Pour 2 inches of oil into a deep skillet, wok, or fryer, and heat it to about 375 degrees F. It is hot enough when a pinch of cornmeal dropped into the oil sizzles on contact.
2. Place the okra in a lidded container or bag with the cornmeal and salt and shake to coat. Remove the okra with your hands, shaking off excess cornmeal.
3. Add as many pods as will fit at a time and fry until crisp and browned, about 3 minutes, then use a slotted spoon or skimmer to transfer the okra to a paper towel–lined plate. Repeat with remaining okra. Serve hot, sprinkled with more salt if you like.

Oven-Fried Okra

ᛤ *Mom Says:* Faith tries to eat healthfully these days, so she asked me to help her come up with a way to prepare okra so it's not deep-fried, but still crunchy and delicious. We both agree that this "guilt-free" version tastes just as good as fried.

SERVES 4

20 pods fresh okra, trimmed and sliced into
    ¹/₂-inch-thick rounds (about 5 cups)
1 cup cornmeal
¹/₂ teaspoon salt
Olive oil, for brushing or spraying

1. Preheat the oven to 375 degrees F.
2. Place the okra in a lidded container or bag with the cornmeal and salt and shake to coat. Remove the okra with your hands, shaking off excess cornmeal.
3. Brush or spray a rimmed baking sheet with oil, then spread the breaded okra evenly in the pan. Lightly spray or drizzle the okra with oil, shaking the pan to coat the okra. Bake, shaking the pan from time to time, until the okra is crisp and browned, about 30 minutes. Serve while hot and crispy, sprinkled with more salt if you like.

Purple Hull Peas

⚜ **Mom Says:** Recently a scientific study confirmed a connection between the foods a pregnant mother craves and the foods her child prefers to eat. I can bear witness to that because that's exactly what happened with me and Faith.

Purple hull peas are a type of field pea grown in the South and elsewhere in the nation where Southerners have settled. The purple hull pea got its name from its distinctive shell, which turns purple when ripe and ready to be picked.

The summer I was pregnant with Faith, the purple hull peas were plentiful. Not so every summer. Sometimes it rains too much, sometimes too little, and sometimes they are badly stung by bugs. This particular summer the peas, tomatoes, and okra were just right. And I craved purple hull peas—I just couldn't seem to get enough!

Faith was born in mid-September, and by the next summer she was eating mashed purple hull peas and *she* just couldn't seem to get enough! Later on she would even concoct purple hull pea sandwiches. I suppose that was her imagination at work with food for the first time.

Our family moved about two hours away to Monroe from our little hometown of Jonesville when Faith was about one year old. Every year the girls would go back to the farm to visit my parents. After the girls got back from one such visit, I had hastily cooked up a pot of purple hull peas for supper. Faith tasted the peas, looked at me seriously and informed me that we needed a new stove, one like Grandma Cora's. She was always the little diplomat—never would she have said that my peas were not as good as my mother's, it had to be the stove. I laughed and informed her that it was not the stove, it was the cook and that she must watch very carefully on her next trip and learn how Grandma cooked the peas. Then she could come back and teach me. Well, with my mother's help and much practice, she did become a purple hull pea expert! I try, but still can't cook purple hull peas as well as Faith.

Grandma Cora's Purple Hull Peas

Purple hull peas are related to black-eyed peas and crowder peas—all considered Southern peas—and grow well in hot weather. The hulls stain your thumbs purple, but everyone agrees it's worth it because a bowl of steaming fresh purple hull peas is so flavorful and tasty. Make sure not to cook away all the rich, amber-colored juice; it's great with cornbread.

Mom Says: Brown field peas are really not a substitute for purple hull peas, but we use them if we don't have any fresh purple hull peas on hand. Or you could substitute black-eyed peas.

SERVES 4

> 1 slice bacon, ham, or turkey tasso (about 1 ounce),
>   cut into quarters
> 1 quart fresh purple hull peas, shelled, or
>   2 cups frozen (see Sources, page 267)
> 1 teaspoon salt

1. Put the bacon, ham, or tasso in a pot with a lid and fry slowly over medium heat until golden brown, about 5 minutes.
2. Add the peas to the pot and carefully pour in enough water to cover them by an inch. Bring to a boil, then reduce the heat to a slow bubbling simmer and cover. Check every 15 minutes and add more water as needed. The juice will darken as the peas cook, but it will remain thin, not thick. Peas cooked too fast or stirred too much will come apart. The peas are done when they are tender to taste but not mushy, 25 to 45 minutes. Season with salt and serve hot with some of the pot liquid. Or you can let them cool, cover, and refrigerate them for up to 2 days, then reheat in their liquid.

Red-Hot Black-Eyed Peas

I like my purple hull peas plain, but I like black-eyed peas dressed up with some spice, plenty of juicy tomatoes, and a little chicken broth for extra flavor. Most of the time I make these with canned diced tomatoes, but if I have some extra fresh salsa in the fridge, I often substitute that. You may want to cut down on the hot sauce if your salsa is on the fiery side, but then again, you may not. Leftovers are perfect for Warm Pasta Salad with Chicken Andouille Sausage, Mustard Greens, and Black-Eyed Peas (page 48) or Black-Eyed Pea Soup with Sausage and Mustard Greens (page 61).

SERVES 6

1 tablespoon olive oil

1 garlic clove, minced or passed through a garlic press

1 pound fresh black-eyed peas, shelled and sorted, 1 (16-ounce) package frozen, or 3 (15-ounce) cans, rinsed and drained

1 cup chicken broth, canned or homemade (page 72), or water

1 (15-ounce) can diced tomatoes, or 1½ cups chunky salsa, preferably fresh (from the prepared foods section of the grocery store)

½ teaspoon salt

¼ teaspoon hot sauce

1. In a wide saucepan over medium-high heat, warm the oil. Add the garlic and sauté for 1 to 2 minutes. Add the peas and broth or water and bring to a boil. Reduce the heat to low, cover, and simmer gently for 10 minutes.

2. Stir in the tomatoes, salt, and hot sauce and simmer until the peas are tender (not mushy) and the sauce is reduced, 10 to 20 minutes. Serve hot. Or you can let them cool, cover, and refrigerate for up to 2 days, then reheat in their liquid.

Southern-Style Green Beans

This is the way my grandma Cora made green beans, simmered long and slow. I liked them growing up because they were nice and soft and had great flavor from the bacon. But nowadays I prefer them a little on the crunchier side, seasoned with soy sauce instead of pork. For my version, see page 160.

⚶ *Mom Says:* When you brown bacon or ham in a pot as a flavoring for greens or beans, you can choose to pour the fat off or leave it in before adding the vegetable. The thing I can't stress enough is that you have to brown the meat before you add anything else. That's where all the good flavor comes from. You can reheat any leftovers for another meal or use them for soup.

SERVES 4

> 1 slice bacon, cut into quarters
> 1 pound fresh green beans, trimmed and snapped in half
> 1 teaspoon salt
> 1 teaspoon sugar

1. Put the bacon in a heavy-bottomed saucepan with a lid and fry slowly over medium heat until golden brown, about 5 minutes.
2. Add the beans along with just enough water to come to the top of the beans. Add the salt and sugar, cover, and cook slowly over low heat until as tender as you like, 10 to 20 minutes. Serve hot or warm with some of the pot liquid.

Green Beans Braised with Balsamic Vinegar and Soy Sauce

When I was growing up, vegetables were cooked until they were perfectly soft—overcooked by today's standard. Even my mom's tastes have changed. These days, she likes me to do my new versions of all our favorite vegetable dishes. She learned to appreciate the crispiness of vegetables cooked until they're just done, not until you could mush them with a fork.

The seasonings here are different from the ones we used when I was growing up, too. Living in New York and Los Angeles introduced me to lots of different ways to flavor foods. That's where the soy sauce comes in. I think of this recipe as a cross between the steamed green beans you get in Chinese restaurants and the flavorful, bacony beans I grew up on.

SERVES 4

> 1 tablespoon olive oil
> 1 pound fresh green beans, trimmed
> 1 tablespoon balsamic vinegar
> 1 tablespoon soy sauce
> Salt and black pepper

Warm the oil in a skillet over medium-high heat. Add the beans and stir around to coat with the hot oil for a minute or two. Add the vinegar and soy sauce and toss to coat the beans well. Reduce the heat to low and cook, covered, for 5 minutes. Check for desired doneness and season with salt and pepper to taste.

Asparagus with Tarragon Vinaigrette

When I was in high school, my mother started growing asparagus. Like corn, asparagus is best eaten the same day it is harvested, so asparagus picked straight from the garden tasted miles better than store-bought. I loved asparagus when I was younger, and it was only later that I found out how good it is for you—as a diuretic, it cleanses your system. Now I have asparagus at least once a week, preferably with plenty of fresh herbs. I especially love it with Ragin' Cajun Roasted Chickens (page 102) or Golden Crispy Oven-Fried Chicken (page 96). It's such a filling vegetable side dish that you don't really miss having rice or pasta as well, and served cold over greens, it makes a great salad.

SERVES 4

> 3 tablespoons chopped fresh tarragon
> 2 tablespoons chopped kalamata or niçoise olives
> 2 tablespoons chopped red onion
> 2 tablespoons white wine vinegar
> 1 teaspoon Creole mustard (see Sources, page 267) or
>   any spicy brown mustard (see Note, page 23)
> ½ cup olive oil
> 2 bunches medium asparagus (about 2 pounds), trimmed
> ½ teaspoon salt

1. In a small bowl, whisk together the tarragon, olives, onion, vinegar, and mustard. Drizzle in the oil, whisking constantly. The dressing can be kept in the refrigerator for up to 4 days.
2. Fill a large covered skillet with 2 inches of water and bring to a boil. Place the asparagus in the skillet and add the salt. Cover and cook to desired doneness, 3 to 5 minutes. Drain in a colander, then rinse under cold running water to stop the cooking. Drain very well.
3. Arrange the asparagus on a platter and drizzle some of the vinaigrette over them. Serve warm, at room temperature, or refrigerate for up to 2 days and serve chilled.

Balsamic-Braised Broccoli

I feel at my best in the morning if I refrain from eating carbohydrates late at night. So, if I'm eating late, especially before a day I'm taping something for television, I'll just do a couple of vegetables, maybe some fish, and a salad. This dish is one of my favorites because it's filling without dragging you down and it's really flavorful on its own.

SERVES 4

> 1 tablespoon balsamic vinegar
> ½ teaspoon Dijon mustard
> ½ teaspoon honey
> 3½ tablespoons olive oil
> 4 garlic cloves, sliced
> 1 large broccoli head, stem peeled, stem and florets
>   cut into pieces (about 5 cups)
> ½ teaspoon salt
> ¼ teaspoon black pepper

1. In a bowl, whisk together the vinegar, mustard, and honey. Whisking constantly, drizzle in 1½ tablespoons of the olive oil. Set aside.
2. In a large (preferably nonstick) pan with a tight-fitting cover, warm the remaining 2 tablespoons olive oil over medium heat. Add the garlic and sauté until lightly browned but not burned, about 2 minutes. Add the broccoli, salt, and pepper and continue to cook, tossing constantly, for 3 minutes.
3. Pour the balsamic mixture over the broccoli, reduce the heat to medium-low, toss well, and cover. Let steam, covered, until the broccoli is bright green and crisp-tender, 7 to 9 minutes. (If the broccoli is sticking and not steaming, add a tablespoon or two of water to the pan and continue to cook, covered.) Serve hot.

Snap Beans and New Potatoes

✤ **Mom Says:** In the South when I was growing up, every farmer planted
potatoes in late February or early March depending upon the weather, so by mid
to late spring the little potatoes were already growing underground. We'd also
sow snap beans in the early spring, just as soon as the danger of frost had passed.

After eating from the stock of old potatoes and canned produce all winter
long, we were all ready for some fresh beans and new potatoes by early summer.
When we couldn't stand it any longer, we'd go "grappling" for potatoes. We'd
take a spading fork and pry around the potato plants, seizing any potatoes that
were the size of a half-dollar. Cooked up with some green beans, those new
potatoes always tasted like spring!

SERVES 4

> 1 pound new potatoes or small red potatoes, halved or quartered if large
> 1 slice bacon, cut into quarters
> 1 teaspoon salt
> 1 teaspoon sugar
> 1 pound fresh green beans, trimmed and snapped in half

1. Scrub the potatoes but do not peel them. Remove the eyes with the tip of a small
   knife. Submerge in water to prevent browning.
2. Put the bacon in a medium saucepan with a lid and fry it slowly over medium heat
   until golden brown, about 5 minutes. Add 3 cups water, the salt, and sugar, cover, and
   bring to a boil.
3. Add the beans and potatoes to the hot broth, cover, and bring back to a boil. (The liquid should just come to the top of the beans and potatoes. Add more water if necessary.) Uncover the pot, reduce the heat to medium, and simmer until the potatoes are
   cooked to fork-tender stage but still firm and intact, about 15 minutes. Drain and
   serve hot.

My Sister's Yellow Squash Casserole

In the South, you can usually still catch the tail end of the summer squash season in late fall. My sister, Devon, takes advantage of the harvest by making this mild and creamy dish every Thanksgiving for all her friends in Nashville, where she now lives. Typically not all our family is together for Thanksgiving—we usually gather for Christmas instead. Since my sister works right up to Thanksgiving Day, she has to do everything at the last minute. This quick dish is festive and colorful, with the red pepper and scallions peeking through the crispy top. When you reheat it, it gets a bit mushy but it's still good.

SERVES 8

> 4 medium yellow squash, cut into ¼-inch slices
> 1½ teaspoons salt
> 3 tablespoons butter
> 1 bunch scallions, chopped (about 1 cup)
> 1 red bell pepper, chopped
> 3 tablespoons all-purpose flour
> 1 cup chicken broth, canned or homemade (page 72)
> ½ cup heavy cream
> ⅓ cup plus 1 tablespoon plain dried bread crumbs
> 1 large egg, beaten
> 1 tablespoon chopped fresh parsley
> 1 tablespoon chopped fresh basil
> ½ teaspoon black pepper

1. Preheat the oven to 350 degrees F.
2. In a large pot, put the squash with water to cover, and ½ teaspoon of the salt. Bring to a boil over high heat, reduce the heat to medium-high, and cook for about 2 minutes, until soft. Drain in a colander and set aside.
3. Return the pot to the stove over medium heat and melt 2 tablespoons of the butter. Add the scallions, bell pepper, and remaining teaspoon of salt and sauté for 5 to 7 minutes, until soft.

4. Add the remaining tablespoon of butter to the pot. Once it has melted, add the flour and mix well. Let cook for about 3 minutes, stirring constantly. Add the chicken broth and quickly stir in; it will thicken almost immediately. Add the squash and mix well. Turn off the heat and add the cream, the ⅓ cup bread crumbs, the egg, chopped fresh herbs, and black pepper.

5. Transfer the mixture to a 2-quart baking dish and sprinkle the remaining tablespoon of bread crumbs on top. Bake for about 40 minutes, until set and lightly browned. Serve immediately.

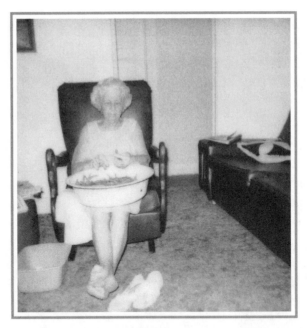

Grandma Cora shelling purple hull peas—my favorite!

Sweet Potato Casserole with Pecan Crumb Topping

A Christmas standard, this has been a tradition in our family for the last twenty years. The whipped potatoes are light and fluffy, like a soufflé, and the sweet pecan crumble topping is the same one we use for our apple pie. I only use fresh sweet potatoes, but my sister uses canned. It tastes exactly the same when it's done, but I have always liked to keep the tradition of using fresh. It's great for big holiday meals because you can make it ahead of time and stick it in the oven right before dinner. When it goes out on the buffet, I put it near the cornbread dressing (pages 174 to 176), and, by the end of the meal, there's usually not a bite of either left.

⤋ *Mom Says:* This can be made with no spices and all white sugar instead of brown sugar if you prefer—it's a matter of taste. The spices make it taste more like sweet potato pie and give it a deeper brown color. Without the spices and with white sugar, it has a brighter color and a more sweet-potato-y flavor.

SERVES 8

Potatoes

   4 medium sweet potatoes (about 2 pounds), peeled and
       cut into 1-inch chunks
   1½ teaspoons salt
   1½ cups half-and-half
   ¾ cup white sugar
   ¼ cup packed brown sugar
   2 large eggs
   1 teaspoon vanilla extract
   1 teaspoon ground cinnamon
   ¼ teaspoon grated nutmeg
   ¼ teaspoon ground cloves

1. Place the potato chunks in a saucepan with water to cover and 1 teaspoon of the salt. Bring to a boil, then cook over medium-high heat for 12 to 15 minutes, until tender when pierced with a fork. Drain and let cool slightly.
2. In the bowl of a standing mixer, combine the potatoes, half-and-half, white sugar, brown sugar, eggs, vanilla, spices, and remaining ½ teaspoon salt and whip just until smooth. Do not overmix.
3. Spread the potato mixture evenly in a 3-quart baking dish and set aside while you prepare the topping. This can be done a day ahead. Cover and refrigerate the potato mixture until ready to sprinkle on the crumb topping and bake.

Crumb Topping
    ½ cup chopped toasted pecans (see page 244)
    ⅓ cup all-purpose flour
    ⅓ cup packed brown sugar
    ½ teaspoon salt
    5 tablespoons butter, melted

1. Preheat the oven to 350 degrees F.
2. In a small bowl, combine the pecans, flour, brown sugar, and salt. Pour on the melted butter and mix until crumbs form.
3. Sprinkle the topping over the potatoes and bake for about 1 hour, until set. Serve hot or warm.

Oven-Roasted Sweet Potatoes

I met Jane Leeves, the British actress, at an acting class in Los Angeles when I first moved there. We became friends and roommates, and she taught me how to cook proper English roasted potatoes. The trick is to parboil them, then roast them in oil. Recently, I decided to try sweet potatoes like that, using fresh rosemary, garlic, and spices. They're good with pork roast (page 136), or whenever I feel I need something with a little sweetness to accompany a main course. I also love their deep, warm color.

SERVES 4

> 3 large sweet potatoes, quartered lengthwise
> ¼ cup olive oil
> 2 tablespoons chopped fresh rosemary
> 1 teaspoon Faith's Special Seasoning (page 266) or
>   Cajun seasoning (see Sources, page 267)
> ½ teaspoon salt
> ¼ teaspoon black pepper
> 6 whole unpeeled garlic cloves

1. Preheat the oven to 400 degrees F.
2. Place the potatoes in a saucepan, cover them with water, and bring to a boil. Cook for 3 to 5 minutes, then drain the potatoes.
3. In a baking pan, mix the oil, rosemary, Faith's seasoning, salt, and pepper. Add the potatoes and garlic and turn to coat with the oil mixture, then spread the potatoes out in one layer.
4. Roast until the potatoes are tender, 25 to 30 minutes, turning them occasionally so all sides get browned. Serve hot or at room temperature.

Cora's Skillet Candied Sweet Potatoes

This is a very old-fashioned recipe from my grandma Cora. It was the thing she brought to potluck suppers. You don't have to have a cast-iron pan to make these, but it does cook the potatoes evenly on all sides. Otherwise, just use a heavy ovenproof skillet and keep your eye on this when you broil it so the sugar doesn't burn.

Mom Says: My mother made great candied sweet potatoes on the stovetop in her big cast-iron skillet, and she probably used about ¼ cup more sugar. I do them in the oven and use a little less sugar because that's how Faith prefers them. I like them both ways.

SERVES 6

> 5 large sweet potatoes, peeled and cut into 2-inch chunks
> ¾ cup plus 2 tablespoons sugar, or more to taste
> ½ teaspoon salt
> 8 tablespoons (1 stick) butter, melted

1. Preheat the oven to 350 degrees F.
2. Arrange the potatoes in a large cast-iron or other heavy ovenproof skillet. Combine the ¾ cup sugar and the salt. Drizzle the butter over the top of the potatoes and sprinkle on the sugar and salt mixture, coating the potatoes well.
3. Place the skillet, uncovered, in the oven for 30 minutes. Remove the skillet, spoon the syrup over the potatoes, carefully flip them, and return the potatoes to the oven for 15 minutes more. Remove the skillet, spoon the syrup over the potatoes again, and return them to the oven until very tender, about another 15 minutes.
4. Remove the skillet and spoon the syrup over the potatoes for a third time. Sprinkle the remaining 2 tablespoons sugar over the potatoes. Switch the oven setting to broil or transfer the pan to the broiler and broil for about 5 minutes, until the sugar coating begins to brown at the edges. Serve warm.

Oven-Baked Sour Cream and Cheese Mashed Potato Casserole

This dish is kind of like twice-baked potatoes, which my mother loves, but it is much easier to make when you're having a large group of people over for dinner. You could assemble it the day before, then just bake it when your guests arrive—no last minute fussing!

⚜ *Mom Says:* Sometimes I sprinkle a teaspoon of cooked, crumbled bacon bits over the top, and it is delicious. I like to serve this with Mom's Smoky Beef Brisket (page 130).

SERVES 8

> 3 baking potatoes, peeled and cut into 1-inch chunks
> 1½ teaspoons salt
> ¼ cup milk or half-and-half
> 1 cup sour cream
> 1½ cups grated cheddar cheese
> 1 bunch scallions, chopped (about 1 cup)
> ½ teaspoon black pepper

1. Preheat the oven to 375 degrees F.
2. In a medium saucepan over medium-high heat, combine the potatoes and 1 teaspoon of the salt and cover with water. Bring to a boil and cook until tender, about 20 minutes.
3. Drain, place in the bowl of an electric mixer, and mix just until fluffy. Do not overmix. Add the milk or half-and-half, sour cream, 1 cup of the cheese, the scallions, the remaining ½ teaspoon salt, and the pepper and mix well.
4. Transfer the mixture to a 2½ quart baking dish and sprinkle with the remaining cheese. At this point you can wrap the dish and refrigerate for up to one day before baking. Bake for 30 to 40 minutes (45 to 55 minutes if the dish was refrigerated), until browned and bubbling on top. Serve warm.

Creamy Irish New Potatoes

My grandma Cora used to make these when the potatoes would come in fresh. Before my grandparents had much money or owned their own cows, they didn't eat a lot of meat, so potatoes were certainly a nice hearty filler—the part of the meal that stuck to your ribs. I still find them comforting. Serve them with sliced ripe summer tomatoes and a green salad.

❧ *Mom Says:* Every farm family had a garden when I was growing up, and we always harvested some new potatoes to check on the size so we could figure out when it would be time to dig the potatoes to store for the year. This is how the new potatoes were prepared, since they were too hard to be fried and too young and waxy to be mashed.

SERVES 4

> 1½ pounds new potatoes, halved or quartered if large
> 1 slice bacon, cut into quarters
> ½ small onion, chopped
> 1 teaspoon salt
> ¼ teaspoon black pepper
> 1 cup milk or half-and-half
> 2 tablespoons all-purpose flour

1. Scrub the potatoes but do not peel them. Remove the eyes with the tip of a small knife. Submerge in water to prevent browning.
2. Put the bacon in a heavy-bottomed pot with a lid and fry it slowly over medium heat until golden brown, about 5 minutes. Add the onion, and sauté for 1 to 2 minutes. Add 1 cup water, the salt, and pepper and bring to a boil. Add the potatoes, cover, and cook over medium heat for 10 to 20 minutes, until the largest potato is just tender when pricked with a fork. Never cook potatoes to the mushy stage.
3. Whisk together the milk or half-and-half and the flour until smooth. Add to the potatoes and stir until the liquid thickens, 3 to 5 minutes. Adjust the salt and pepper to suit your family's taste and serve immediately.

Dilled Rice with Corn and Garlic

This dressed up rice dish is best served alongside fish and I especially like it with Cajun Better 'n Blackened Catfish (page 85). The green feathery dill, sweet yellow corn, and delicately flavored basmati rice give the dish a light and clean taste. You can jazz up this dish further by throwing in some sugar snap peas or any other vegetable or herb you like.

SERVES 4

> 1½ cups chicken or vegetable broth, canned or
> homemade (pages 72 to 73) or water
> 1 cup basmati rice, rinsed
> 3 tablespoons chopped fresh dill
> 2 tablespoons olive oil
> ½ teaspoon salt
> ½ teaspoon black pepper
> 3 garlic cloves, chopped
> ½ cup sweet white or yellow corn kernels (from ½ ear fresh corn), or
> ¼ (10-ounce) package frozen kernels
> 1 tablespoon capers or chopped dill pickle

1. In a medium heavy-bottomed saucepan over high heat, combine the broth or water, rice, 1 tablespoon of the chopped dill, 1 tablespoon of the olive oil, salt, and pepper. Cover and bring to a boil. Reduce the heat to medium-low and simmer, covered, for about 15 minutes, stirring occasionally.

2. When the rice is done, stir in the remaining 2 tablespoons chopped dill. Replace the lid and set aside.

3. In a small nonstick pan over medium heat, warm the remaining tablespoon of oil. Add the garlic and sauté for 2 to 3 minutes, until lightly browned but not burned. Add the corn and sauté for 1 minute more. Remove from the heat, stir in the capers or pickle, and toss with the rice. Keep covered until ready to serve, up to 4 hours, or refrigerate for up to 2 days. Serve warm or at room temperature.

Three Hens in the Kitchen

Thanksgiving and Christmastime were always a huge deal in my family. Mom, Aunt Brenda, and Grandma Cora spent days cooking and getting ready. By the time they were done, there was so much food you could hardly fit it all on the table! Each one made her own special main dishes. Mama would roast a turkey. Aunt Brenda would smoke one. And Grandma Cora baked a fresh ham. But there was one dish that they all collaborated on—cornbread dressing. This was the real centerpiece of the meal: fluffy and moist with a puffed up, golden brown top.

The dressing was always made at the last minute because you wanted to have it right out of the oven. It didn't taste as good if it cooled. So just before we sat down to dinner, while the men were in the living room talking and the kids were in front of the TV watching the parade if it was Thanksgiving, we would all hear Mama, Aunt Brenda, and Grandma Cora in the kitchen, making the dressing.

Or, to tell the whole truth, arguing about the dressing.

No matter how many years they made it together, they never could agree on the best method. They each had strong opinions about how much broth should be put in, or how much to stir it, or how long to cook it. One cook would put the broth in, and the other would say "that's too much" or "when did you stir it last?" and "well, I told you I put enough in there" or "it seems dry" or "don't burn the dressing!" and on and on. They'd be deep into it, and the men would listen to the little bits of conversation drifting in from the kitchen and laugh. They'd say, "Sounds just like three hens cackling!" So that's what we would call them, three hens in the kitchen.

But you know what? It was always perfect.

Three Hens' Cornbread Dressing

Here's my family's traditional version of cornbread dressing. It's rich and soft and savory, almost a meal in itself, but of course best when served with turkey or ham. When I was growing up, we always used the whole hard-boiled egg, but nowadays we sometimes only use the whites. You can do it either way.

SERVES 12

Chicken and Broth

    1 chicken (about 3½ pounds), cut into 8 pieces
    1 small onion, chopped
    4 celery stalks, chopped
    2 teaspoons salt
    1 teaspoon black pepper

1. Combine all the ingredients along with 8 cups water in a large pot and bring to a boil. Reduce the heat and simmer for 45 minutes.
2. Remove the chicken and skim any fat from the broth. Cool and strain through a colander set over a large bowl. Reserve the broth, onion and celery, and chicken separately.
3. Pull the chicken meat from the bone and save the chicken for sandwiches or pot pies. (This can all be done the day before. Cover and refrigerate the broth and the onion-celery mixture until ready to assemble the dressing.)

Dressing

    6 cups crumbled homemade cornbread, made without sugar (page 198)
    3 slices white bread, crusts removed, torn into pieces
    6 large eggs, hard-boiled (see page 9), peeled, and chopped
    1 bunch scallions, chopped (about 1 cup)
    2 celery stalks, chopped
    Salt and black pepper
    3 whole raw eggs
    4 tablespoons (½ stick) butter, melted

Blackberry Pancakes with
Blackberry Syrup (page 189)

Smoked Turkey and Avocado Po' Boys with Sweet Tangy Mayo (page 16), Pleasingly Purple Cabbage Salad with Basil Balsamic Dressing (page 39), and Fresh Mint Iced Tea (page 210)

Crispy Oven-Fried Chicken
Breasts (page 98) and Warm
Black-Eyed Pea Salad (page 46)

**Dinner-on-the-Ground
Chicken 'n' Dumplin's (page 100)**

**Smoky Turkey Roast (page 110,
Three Hens' Cornbread Dressing (page 174),
and Balsamic-Braised Broccoli (page 162)**

Citrus-Roasted Pork Loin (page 138),
Warm Corn Salad with Bacon and Sage (page 47),
and Faith's Double "S" Mustard Greens (page 151)

Mama's Vegetable Beef Soup (page 64),
Sit-Down Sizzlin' Salad (page 31), and
Spicy Cornbread Muffins with Fresh
White Corn (page 201)

Grandma Cora's Fluffy
Catahoula Coconut Cake (page 248)

1. Preheat the oven to 400 degrees F.
2. Combine the cornbread and white bread in a Dutch oven or roasting pan. Add the reserved celery and onion (from the chicken broth), the chopped egg, and 4 cups of the hot chicken broth. Stir well and let the liquid be absorbed.
3. Add the scallions, celery, and 2 cups more chicken broth. Mix well, taste, and add salt and pepper if desired, then mix in the raw eggs. At this point the mixture should be a little soupy—add more stock if necessary.
4. Bake, covered (with foil if using a roasting pan), for 30 minutes. Remove from the oven and stir away from the sides of the pan into the center to ensure even cooking. Drizzle the butter over the top and return, uncovered, to the oven. Bake for 30 to 45 minutes more, until the top is golden and the sides are bubbly. Serve hot with gravy made from the roast turkey drippings.

Faith's Herbed Cornbread Dressing with Sausage, White Corn, and Scallions

My recipe for cornbread dressing is faster and easier than the one my mother, Aunt Brenda, and Grandma Cora always made. It's also stress-free—since it's my kitchen, there's no arguing! If you want to heat up leftovers, add a few tablespoons of broth and cook the dressing slowly so it doesn't dry out. If you can't find white corn, yellow corn works just as well.

SERVES 12

2 tablespoons olive oil

½ pound turkey sausage, casings removed

4 celery stalks, chopped

1 small onion, chopped

2 cups sweet white or yellow corn kernels (from 2 ears fresh corn), or
    1 (10-ounce) package frozen kernels

6 cups crumbled cornbread, purchased or homemade (page 201)

3 slices white bread, crusts removed, torn into pieces

1 bunch scallions, chopped (about 1 cup)

1 tablespoon chopped fresh sage

1 tablespoon chopped fresh thyme leaves

1 tablespoon chopped fresh oregano or basil

1 tablespoon chopped fresh parsley

5 to 6 cups chicken broth, canned or homemade (page 72)

1 cup evaporated skim milk

Salt and black pepper

3 large egg whites, beaten

4 tablespoons (½ stick) butter, melted

1. Preheat the oven to 350 degrees F.
2. Warm the olive oil in a skillet over medium-high heat. Add the sausage and brown for 5 minutes. Add the celery and onion and cook until the meat is no longer pink and the vegetables are softened, about 7 minutes. Stir in the corn.
3. In a Dutch oven or roasting pan, combine the cornbread, white bread, sausage mixture, scallions, and herbs. Pour 5 cups of the broth over all and stir to combine. Let sit for 15 minutes, then add the evaporated milk and salt and pepper to taste. The mixture should be a little thinner than pancake batter—add more broth if necessary. Pour the egg whites over the dressing and mix well.
4. Cover (with foil if using a roasting pan) and bake for 30 minutes. Remove from the oven and stir well. Drizzle the butter over the top and stir to incorporate the butter. Bake uncovered for another 30 to 45 minutes or until golden brown but not dry. Serve hot.

Devon's Wild Rice and Sage-Sausage Dressing

One year, my sister, Devon, decided she didn't like cornbread dressing. She said she had never liked it in the first place, but I always remember her eating it! Well, my sister is set in her ways and she insisted that she just could not eat cornbread dressing anymore. So she came up with this brown rice and wild rice dressing. Now it's a family tradition to have both. Personally, I prefer the traditional cornbread dressing, but I like hers, too, which does have an amazing, nutty, herby flavor. It goes well with Ragin' Cajun Roasted Chickens (page 102) or as a side dish at a barbecue.

SERVES 12

5 tablespoons vegetable oil

1 pound pork or turkey sausage, casing removed

1 pound ground turkey breast

2 tablespoons Faith's Special Seasoning (page 266) or
   Cajun seasoning (see Sources, page 267)

1 bunch scallions, chopped (about 1 cup)

1 green bell pepper, chopped

2 celery stalks, chopped

1 tablespoon chopped fresh sage

1 tablespoon chopped fresh parsley

1 tablespoon fresh thyme, or 2 teaspoons dried thyme

3 tablespoons all-purpose flour

2 cups chicken broth, canned or homemade (page 72)

Salt and black pepper

4½ cups cooked brown rice (from about 1½ cups raw rice,
   cooked according to package directions)

5 cups wild rice or wild rice blend (from about 1½ cups raw rice,
   cooked according to package directions)

3 tablespoons plain dried bread crumbs

1 teaspoon sweet paprika

1. Preheat the oven to 350 degrees F.
2. In a heavy skillet over medium-high heat, warm 2 tablespoons of the oil. Cook the meat, stirring to break it up, until it begins to brown, about 5 minutes. Add Faith's seasoning and continue to cook until the meat is no longer pink, about 5 more minutes. If the meat begins to stick to the bottom of the pan as it cooks, add a few tablespoons of water.
3. When the meat is almost cooked, add 1 tablespoon of the oil to a Dutch oven or other heavy-bottomed, deep pot set over medium-high heat. Add the scallions, bell pepper, and celery and sauté until the vegetables are limp, but not brown, 5 to 7 minutes. Turn off the heat and add the cooked meat and the herbs.
4. Scrape up the debris from the skillet and add the remaining 2 tablespoons oil and the flour. With the heat on medium-high, cook the mixture for 1 to 2 minutes, stirring. Add the chicken broth and bring to a simmer, stirring as it thickens. It will be somewhat like cream of chicken soup. Season this mixture with salt and pepper. Turn off the heat.
5. Add the cooked rice to the Dutch oven and mix well. Add the thickened chicken broth mixture from the skillet, stir well, and adjust the seasoning to taste. Transfer the mixture to a large rectangular baking dish, sprinkle with bread crumbs and paprika, and bake for 25 to 30 minutes, until golden on top. Serve warm.

CHAPTER 8

Breakfasts, Breads, and Beverages

Creamy Cheese Grits

Growing up, my sister and I ate breakfast at school. In the cafeteria, they'd make big pans of grits with plenty of butter in them. If you had the right people cooking, they'd keep them well stirred and smooth. But sometimes a crust would form on top—then you'd have lumps in the middle, and I never liked that.

At home, my mother designated me grits maker because I was so particular about keeping them lump free. The trick is to stir as you pour in the grits, since that's when the lumps form. We always made our grits into cheese grits by melting in whatever cheese we had around.

I like my grits a bit thinner than average (so you can serve them in a bowl, not a plate) and I make them flavorful. I use a little less cheese than we did when I was a kid, and add milk and cottage cheese as well, which give the grits a creamy consistency and some calcium.

Be sure not to let your grits sit and congeal if you're serving them hot—either you have to eat them right away, or you can let them get cold and make things out of them, like Cheese Grits Croutons (page 34).

⤜ *Mom Says:* Try sliced tomatoes with these grits. They also go well with scrambled eggs, turkey sausage, and toast.

SERVES 4

> 1 teaspoon salt
> ½ cup grits
> 2 tablespoons butter, optional
> 1 cup grated extra-sharp cheddar cheese
> ½ cup cottage cheese
> ½ cup milk
> Black pepper

1. In a medium saucepan, bring 2 cups of water to a boil, add the salt, then slowly add the grits, stirring to prevent lumping. Reduce the heat to low and simmer, uncovered, stirring frequently, until the grits thicken, 10 to 15 minutes.
2. Stir in the butter, if using. Add the cheddar cheese, cottage cheese, milk, and salt and pepper to taste. Stir until the cheese melts. Serve hot.

Country Cheese and Herb Grits Frittata

This is a lighter version of the grits casserole my mom used to make for company.

SERVES 6

> 2 cups milk
> 2 teaspoons salt
> 1 cup grits
> 2 tablespoons olive oil
> 2 scallions, chopped
> ¼ cup chopped fresh parsley
> 1 cup grated Parmesan cheese
> 1 teaspoon Dijon mustard
> ½ teaspoon black pepper
> 3 large eggs
> 3 large egg whites

1. Preheat the oven to 375 degrees F.
2. Put 1½ cups of the milk, 1½ cups water, and 1 teaspoon of the salt in a medium saucepan and bring to a low boil over medium-high heat, making sure not to scorch the mixture. As soon as the liquid starts to bubble, slowly add the grits, stirring constantly to prevent lumps. Reduce the heat to medium and simmer for 8 to 10 minutes, stirring frequently.
3. Meanwhile, in a large ovenproof skillet (I like using a well-seasoned cast-iron skillet) over high heat, warm the oil. Add the scallions and sauté for 1 minute. Add the parsley and sauté for another minute. Turn off the heat.
4. Add the cheese, mustard, and pepper to the grits, stirring well. In a mixing bowl, whisk together the remaining ½ cup milk, the eggs, egg whites, and remaining 1 teaspoon salt. Pour the egg mixture into the skillet. Pour in the grits and mix in with a fork, making sure to break up any lumps that have formed. Place the skillet in the oven and bake for 25 to 30 minutes, until the frittata has puffed up and is beginning to brown on top. Serve hot.

Smoked Salmon–Egg White Scramble

Egg whites and smoked salmon are definitely not Southern. I first discovered smoked salmon when I worked as a hostess at a Jewish deli in New York. Who would have thought of having fish in the morning? But I don't really think of it as having fish—my Southern way of looking at it is as a substitute for bacon.

For egg white omelets and scrambles, I usually buy a carton of egg whites. If you do separate your own eggs for this recipe, don't throw out the yolks. I always hear my mom in my ear if I go to throw away a yolk: "Faith, don't waste that yolk. Save it and use it later!" You can freeze yolks, in a tightly sealed container, for up to three months. You can use them in all kinds of things, like ice cream and custard.

SERVES 4

2 tablespoons olive oil
½ small red onion, chopped
3 scallions, chopped
1 tablespoon capers
2 cups egg whites, whisked together
    (from 16 eggs or 2 cups packaged egg whites)
4 ounces smoked salmon, chopped
1 teaspoon black pepper
½ teaspoon hot sauce
½ teaspoon salt, or to taste
1 tablespoon chopped fresh dill
Sliced tomatoes

1. In a nonstick skillet over medium heat, warm the olive oil. Add the red onion and sauté for 2 to 3 minutes, until tender. Add the scallions and sauté for 1 minute more. Add the capers, followed by the egg whites, salmon, pepper, hot sauce, and salt. Stir from the outside in until the eggs cook through, about 10 minutes.
2. Fold in the fresh dill and serve with sliced tomatoes.

Dilled Egg White Salad

I first got used to the idea of just using egg whites for egg salad on the set of *Murphy Brown,* when I was trying to concoct a healthy breakfast for Candice Bergen and myself. I'd scoop out the doughy part of a bagel, toast the crust, and then fill it with chopped hard-boiled egg whites. I'd add just a little mayo and some capers, dill, and chopped fresh tomatoes, and there was a tasty and nutritious morning meal.

This dish is definitely a California thing—if I were in Louisiana, I'd be putting in those yolks. If you're not sure about eating only egg whites, try adding half the yolks to this recipe.

SERVES 3

> 6 large eggs, hard-boiled (see page 9) and cooled
> 4 teaspoons chopped fresh dill
> 1 tablespoon regular or light mayonnaise
> 1 tablespoon capers
> 2 teaspoons Dijon mustard
> Salt and black pepper

1. Slice the hard-boiled eggs in half, scoop out the yolks, and reserve them for another use. Chop the whites.
2. In a bowl, combine the dill, mayonnaise, capers, mustard, and salt and pepper to taste, and mix well. Stir in the chopped egg whites. Serve immediately, or cover and refrigerate overnight.

Honey-Peanut Granola

With all the traveling we do, Campion and I are becoming experts at cross-country driving, and granola is perfect for road trips. It's not only great as a breakfast cereal, it makes a good snack. I also like to have a bowl of granola with yogurt, cottage cheese, or milk before bed— the calcium in the dairy helps me go to sleep. I don't put dried fruits in my granola because I like to eat it with fresh berries from the garden, or sliced peaches, apples, or bananas.

⁂ *Mom Says:* Here's a tip you can use for all the granola recipes and any other time you're dealing with sticky ingredients. Measure the honey and syrup into the same measuring cup you've just used for the oil. The coating of oil will prevent the gooey stuff from sticking to the cup, and it'll just slide right out. Coating your spatula with oil before mixing everything together will also make your life easier.

MAKES 7 CUPS

4 cups old-fashioned rolled oats
2 cups raw peanuts
½ teaspoon salt
½ teaspoon ground cinnamon
¼ teaspoon grated nutmeg
½ cup vegetable oil
½ cup honey
3 tablespoons light or dark molasses or cane syrup (see Sources, page 267)

1. Preheat the oven to 350 degrees F. Position a rack in the middle of the oven.
2. In a large bowl, combine the oats, peanuts, salt, cinnamon, and nutmeg. Pour the oil, honey, and molasses or cane syrup over the dry mixture and stir together until the oats and nuts are evenly coated.
3. Spread the mixture out evenly in two 9-by-12-inch baking pans and bake for 30 to 35 minutes, until lightly browned. Make sure to turn the mixture with a spatula every 10 minutes.
4. Remove the granola from the oven and turn it from time to time as it cools and crisps. Wait until it is completely cool before transferring it to a covered container. The granola will keep up to 3 months.

Mixed Nut Granola

You can use any combination of nuts in this recipe, which I like to think of as my "basic blend." The sunflower seeds are rich in iron and the wheat germ adds protein to make this granola especially healthful.

MAKES 7 CUPS

> 4 cups old-fashioned rolled oats
> ¼ cup wheat germ
> ¼ cup pecans, coarsely chopped
> ¼ cup raw peanuts
> ¼ cup walnuts, coarsely chopped
> ¼ cup slivered blanched almonds
> ¼ cup raw sunflower seeds
> ½ teaspoon salt
> ½ teaspoon ground cinnamon
> ¼ teaspoon grated nutmeg
> ½ cup vegetable oil
> ¼ cup honey
> ¼ cup maple syrup
> 2 tablespoons light or dark molasses or cane syrup (see Sources, page 267)

1. Preheat the oven to 350 degrees F. Position a rack in the middle of the oven.
2. In a large bowl, combine the oats, wheat germ, pecans, peanuts, walnuts, almonds, sunflower seeds, salt, cinnamon, and nutmeg. Pour the oil, honey, maple syrup, and molasses or cane syrup over the dry mixture and stir together until the oats and nuts are evenly coated.
3. Spread the mixture out evenly in two 9-by-12-inch baking pans and bake for 30 to 35 minutes, until lightly browned. Make sure to turn the mixture with a spatula every 10 minutes.
4. Remove the granola from the oven and turn it from time to time as it cools and crisps. Wait until it is completely cool before transferring it to a covered container. The granola will keep for up to 3 months.

Maple-Pecan Granola

The maple syrup in this granola variation makes it perfect as a topping for Faith's Peach and Granola Crumble (see page 217). You can substitute walnuts or almonds for the pecans if you like.

MAKES 7 CUPS

4 cups old-fashioned rolled oats

1½ cups coarsely chopped pecans

¼ cup wheat germ

½ teaspoon salt

½ teaspoon ground cinnamon

½ teaspoon grated nutmeg

½ cup vegetable oil

½ cup maple syrup

3 tablespoons molasses

1. Preheat the oven to 350 degrees F. Position a rack in the middle of the oven.
2. In a large bowl, combine the oats, pecans, wheat germ, salt, cinnamon, and nutmeg. Pour the oil, maple syrup, and molasses over the dry mixture and stir together until the oats and nuts are evenly coated.
3. Spread the mixture out evenly in two 9-by-12-inch baking pans and bake for 30 to 35 minutes, until lightly browned. Make sure to turn the mixture with a spatula every 10 minutes.
4. Remove the granola from the oven and turn it from time to time as it cools and crisps. Wait until it is completely cool before transferring it to a covered container. The granola will keep for up to 3 months.

Blackberry Pancakes with Blackberry Syrup

We loved having pancakes on the weekends, and when blackberries were in season, there was nothing better than these. Out of season, frozen blackberries work well, too—just make sure to thaw them first. If you want to gild the lily, you can serve the pancakes with homemade blackberry syrup. But if that's too much trouble, maple syrup is great.

❧ Mom Says: The cinnamon in this recipe was Faith's idea, and it works great with the blackberry flavor. It won't hurt the pancakes if you leave it out, but do try it once unless you really don't like cinnamon.

MAKES ABOUT 12 PANCAKES, SERVING 4

1½ cups all-purpose flour
2 tablespoons packed light or dark brown sugar
1½ teaspoons baking powder
1 teaspoon ground cinnamon, optional
½ teaspoon salt
1 cup milk
2 large eggs
1 cup blackberries, thawed if frozen
Melted butter or vegetable oil, for frying
Blackberry Syrup (page 259) or maple syrup, for serving

1. In a medium bowl, combine the flour, brown sugar, baking powder, cinnamon, and salt. In a small bowl, beat together the milk and eggs. Add the wet ingredients to the dry ingredients and whisk gently to combine. Fold in the blackberries.
2. Preheat the oven to 150 degrees F. Heat a griddle or large skillet over medium-high heat.
3. Add a thin coating of butter or vegetable oil to the griddle. Spoon ⅓ cup of batter onto the griddle for each pancake and cook for 1 to 2 minutes per side. Transfer the pancakes to an ovenproof plate and place in the oven to keep warm. Add additional butter or oil to the griddle as needed to cook the remaining pancakes. Serve with the blackberry syrup for a double delight, or maple syrup.

Down-Home Biscuits

Biscuits are a real comfort food in the South. It's great to wake up in the morning and smell them baking in the oven. My send-off breakfast, whenever I leave Louisiana, is biscuits with eggs, sausage, and grits. When I was growing up, we usually had fresh biscuits on the weekends. Any leftovers would be toasted the next day and smeared with peanut butter and syrup, or topped with melted cheese or sausage. And whenever we felt tired and lazy, we'd make biscuits for lunch or dinner—or even for dessert.

I grew up on all kinds of biscuits. My mother makes drop ones, plop ones, and rolled out and cut ones. She'll sometimes just take a loose spoonful of dough and form the biscuit a little, then coat it in oil on both sides and plop it in a skillet. When you nestle them right up against each other, they all bake up together. Break them apart, and they're soft and steamy on the inside, crunchy on the bottom.

Biscuits are always a good idea for entertaining because there are so many ways to make them. They can be plain or sweet, or you can add herbs or grated cheese or little bits of meat to make them savory. You can also make them in any shape or size. For a dinner party, you can cut out tiny rounds for mini biscuits or bake them in mini muffin tins. Any way you cut them, fresh hot biscuits taste so good and always take me back home.

Skillet Drop Biscuits with Variations

Baking these biscuits in a hot, greased cast-iron skillet makes them crunchy and nicely browned on the bottom, while they stay fluffy and soft inside. You can also use a preheated, greased baking sheet or 10-inch cake pan instead. Just keep in mind when laying out the biscuits in a skillet or pan that when they are positioned so they touch each other, they will bake higher, thicker, and softer. When placed in the skillet or pan without touching, they tend to spread more and are a little crispier all over, like scones.

⚶ *Mom Says:* When you make biscuits, be sure to sift your flour twice, before measuring it into the bowl. You'll end up with lighter, fluffier biscuits.

MAKES 8 (3-INCH) BISCUITS PER RECIPE

> 6 tablespoons unsalted butter, plus additional for brushing, optional
> 2 cups sifted self-rising flour (see Note, page 192)
> ¾ cup milk, plus additional for brushing, optional

1. Preheat the oven to 450 degrees F.
2. Melt 5 tablespoons of the butter in a small saucepan over medium heat, or in the microwave. Place a medium skillet, preferably cast iron, in the oven to heat up.
3. Place the flour in a bowl and make a well in the center. In a small bowl, whisk together the milk and melted butter. Pour the wet ingredients into the well in the flour and use a fork to fold them together. Do not overmix.
4. Add the remaining tablespoon butter to the hot skillet about a minute before you are ready to bake the biscuits. Remove the skillet from the oven and turn the pan to coat with the melted butter. Use an oil-coated spoon or your hands to scoop 8 portions of the dough into the skillet. Brush the tops with milk or melted butter if you like. Bake for 10 minutes.
5. Switch the oven setting to broil or transfer the pan to the broiler and broil for 2 to 3 minutes, until the tops brown. Serve immediately.

NOTE: It's easy to make your own self-rising flour, just remember to sift before measuring flour for biscuits. For each cup needed combine 1 cup minus 2 teaspoons sifted all-purpose flour with 1½ teaspoons baking powder and ½ teaspoon salt.

Buttermilk Biscuits

½ cup vegetable oil, or 8 tablespoons (1 stick) melted unsalted butter, plus
    1 tablespoon oil or butter for skillet
½ teaspoon baking soda
2 cups sifted self-rising flour (see Note, above)
½ cup buttermilk

Follow the directions for Skillet Drop Biscuits (page 191), mixing the baking soda into the flour, and substituting buttermilk for the milk.

Cheese Biscuits

½ cup vegetable oil, or 8 tablespoons (1 stick) melted unsalted butter, plus
    1 tablespoon oil or butter for skillet
½ teaspoon baking soda
2 cups sifted self-rising flour (see Note, above)
½ cup buttermilk
⅔ cup shredded cheese such as cheddar or Parmesan, or a combination

Follow the directions for Skillet Drop Biscuits (page 191), mixing the baking soda into the flour, substituting buttermilk for the milk, and adding the cheese to the dry ingredients before folding everything together.

Cinnamon Raisin Biscuits

½ cup raisins
½ cup vegetable oil, or 8 tablespoons (1 stick) melted unsalted butter, plus
    1 tablespoon oil or butter for skillet
1 tablespoon brown sugar
1 teaspoon ground cinnamon

2 cups sifted self-rising flour (see Note, page 192)
¼ cup buttermilk
¼ cup milk

Plump the raisins by covering them with hot water and letting them sit for 10 to 15 minutes. Drain well. Follow the directions for Skillet Drop Biscuits (page 191), using both buttermilk and regular milk and adding the plumped raisins, brown sugar, and cinnamon to the flour before folding together.

Sausage Surprise Biscuits

½ cup vegetable oil, or 8 tablespoons (1 stick) melted unsalted butter, plus
    1 tablespoon oil or butter for skillet
½ teaspoon baking soda
2 tablespoons chopped fresh herbs, such as sage or parsley, optional
2 cups sifted self-rising flour (see Note, page 192)
½ cup buttermilk
8 (¼-inch-thick) slices turkey or pork breakfast sausage, cooked according to
    package directions

Follow the directions for Skillet Drop Biscuits (page 191), mixing the baking soda and optional herbs, if using, into the flour and substituting buttermilk for the milk. After the biscuits have been placed in the skillet, push a slice of cooked sausage into the center of each. Leaving a little sausage poking through is fine—the dough will rise and pop over the sausage as it bakes.

Cream Cheese and Chive Biscuits

These biscuits are moist, buttery, and slightly tangy from the cream cheese. They go great with Smoked Salmon–Egg White Scramble (page 184) for a delicious weekend brunch. If you like, substitute vegetable oil for some or all of the butter.

MAKES 8 BISCUITS

> 2 cups sifted self-rising flour (see Note, page 192)
> $\frac{1}{2}$ cup (4 ounces) cream cheese
> 4 tablespoons ($\frac{1}{2}$ stick) unsalted butter
> $\frac{3}{4}$ cup milk
> 1 heaping tablespoon chopped fresh chives

1. Preheat the oven to 450 degrees F. Place a heavy skillet, preferably cast iron, on the top rack.
2. In a medium bowl, combine the flour, cream cheese, and 1 tablespoon of the butter. Cut together with a pastry blender or two knives until the mixture has a cornmeal consistency. Add the milk and chives and gently stir together until just combined. Alternatively, pulse together the flour, cream cheese, and 1 tablespoon of the butter in a food processor until a cornmeal consistency is reached. Pulse in the milk and chives until combined.
3. Place 2 tablespoons of the butter in the skillet to heat.
4. Drop heaping spoonfuls of the batter into the skillet to form 8 biscuits. Bake for 10 to 15 minutes, until light golden brown. Melt the remaining 1 tablespoon of butter and brush it on the tops of the biscuits while they are still warm. Serve immediately.

Granola Biscuits

Since I make my own granola, I always have some around the house. One of my favorite ways to eat it is when it's baked into these lightly sweet biscuits. I make them in muffin tins, which is a little twist on the traditional drop or rolled biscuits, and helps them keep a nice shape. For a brunch party, bake them in mini muffin tins (reducing the baking time to 12 minutes) so guests can just pop them into their mouths. They're irresistible, especially when served warm with softened butter.

MAKES 1½ DOZEN BISCUITS

> 3 cups sifted self-rising flour (see Note, page 192)
> 1½ cups granola (preferably homemade, pages 186 to 188)
> ½ cup cane syrup (see Sources, page 267) or maple syrup
> 2 tablespoons unsalted butter
> 1¼ cups milk
> 1 large egg
> ½ teaspoon vanilla extract
> Ground cinnamon

1. Preheat the oven to 375 degrees F. Grease two muffin tins or a baking pan.
2. In a large bowl, combine the flour and granola.
3. In a small microwave-proof bowl or in a saucepan over medium heat, combine the syrup and butter and melt in the microwave, about 45 seconds, or on the stovetop, about 2 minutes.
4. In a medium bowl, whisk together the syrup mixture, milk, egg, and vanilla. Add the wet ingredients to the dry ingredients and fold together. Do not overmix.
5. Spoon the mixture into the muffin tins or, if you are using baking pans, shape the dough into a rectangle on a floured surface, cut into 18 pieces, and place them on the pans. Lightly sprinkle the tops of the biscuits with cinnamon. Bake for 18 to 25 minutes, until golden. Serve immediately or that same day.

Mom's Angel Biscuits

I love these tender biscuits; the yeast makes them a little breadier than the regular kind. Butter and jam, or cane syrup (see Sources, page 267), are a must with these, especially when you serve them warm from the oven.

⚜ *Mom Says:* I have three or four yeast biscuit recipes in my repertoire, including these, which were passed on to my mother by a cousin of ours. The buttermilk gives these biscuits a distinctive tang. Be sure not to skip the sifting step, and these biscuits will be very light and good. The dough can be made ahead, then refrigerated overnight (extra dough can be kept in the refrigerator for up to 1 week) for next morning's breakfast.

MAKES 16 BISCUITS

> 1 package active dry yeast (2¼ teaspoons)
> 4 cups sifted all-purpose flour
> ¼ cup sugar
> 1 tablespoon baking powder
> 1¼ teaspoons baking soda
> 1 teaspoon salt
> 1 cup solid vegetable shortening
> 2 cups buttermilk
> 2 tablespoons unsalted butter, melted

1. Preheat the oven to 375 degrees F. Place a baking sheet on the top rack.
2. In a small bowl, dissolve the yeast in 2 tablespoons warm water. Set aside.
3. In a large bowl, whisk together the flour, sugar, baking powder, baking soda, and salt. Add the shortening and cut it in with a pastry blender or two knives until the mixture has a cornmeal consistency. Add the buttermilk and dissolved yeast and mix well. Alternatively, place the dry ingredients in a food processor and pulse to combine. Add the shortening and pulse until the mixture has a cornmeal consistency. Add the buttermilk and yeast and pulse until the dough comes together in a ball.
4. Turn the dough out onto a well-floured surface. Knead it a few times and press or roll it out to about ½ inch thickness. Use a 3-inch cookie cutter or the rim of a drink-

ing glass to cut out the biscuits. (Extra biscuit dough can be covered and refrigerated for up to 1 week; or the dough can be made the night before and refrigerated until morning.)

5. Spread the melted butter on the preheated baking sheet. Dip each biscuit top first in the butter then flip. Bake for about 12 minutes, until the tops are lightly browned. Serve warm with butter and jam.

An afternoon by the bayou:
Devon and me sitting on one of Grandma Cora's quilts.

Mom's Southern-Style Cornbread

Cornbread was always present at a meal, and, like any Southern bread, was really there to sop up the gravy or pot liquor from a heaping plate of greens. Whenever we had anything that was vaguely juicy or soupy, mom would make cornbread to go with it. I'd take at least two pieces and put one in the bowl to soak up the juice, then I'd just eat the soaked pieces with a spoon. I'd use the other piece to help push stuff onto my fork. Well, that's how we ate in the South.

Watching my mother make cornbread is always so funny to me. Like my grandma Cora, she just hates precise measurements. Instead, she uses a regular serving spoon and she just counts. She'll say, "one-two-three-four-five-six," and that's the cornmeal. Then the flour is "one-two-three." That gives you a fairly dense cornbread. If she wants one that's lighter, then she'll just back off on the cornmeal and add more flour.

🍴 *Mom Says:* This cornbread is best when it's still warm from the oven. Serve the wedges with soups, vegetables, or a glass of cold milk or cold buttermilk (an acquired taste), with butter to spread on while it's warm. This bread is the base for Three Hens' Cornbread Dressing (page 174). Just be sure to leave out the sugar when making cornbread for dressing. If you are making it for the dressing, the cornbread can be made a day ahead.

SERVES 8

 2 cups yellow cornmeal, plus additional for the pan
 1 cup all-purpose flour
 1 tablespoon baking powder
 2 teaspoons sugar
 1 teaspoon salt
 1 large egg
 1¼ cups milk
 3 to 4 tablespoons vegetable oil or melted bacon drippings

1. Preheat the oven to 400 degrees F.
2. In a large bowl, whisk together the cornmeal, flour, baking powder, sugar, and salt. In another bowl, beat the egg with the milk. Pour the wet ingredients over the dry ingre-

dients and mix until just smooth. Fold the mixture a few more times for a lighter cornbread.

3. Pour vegetable oil or bacon drippings into a large skillet, preferably cast iron, or a 9-by-12-inch baking pan. Place the skillet or pan in the oven for 5 minutes. Carefully remove the skillet or pan from the oven, swirl the oil over the bottom and onto the sides to coat, and sprinkle in cornmeal to coat the bottom. Scrape in the batter and use a rubber spatula to smooth the oil that rises on the sides over the top of the batter (this helps form a nice crust).

4. Bake for 20 to 25 minutes until the top is golden brown and springs back when lightly pressed. Let the cornbread cool for 10 minutes then turn it onto a plate and cut it into wedges to serve. If using a 9-by-12-inch pan, cut the bread into squares in the pan.

Cows, Biscuits, and Cornbread

My grandma and grandpa Ford used to have a great old dairy cow that gave them gallons and gallons of milk every day. It was my dad's job to milk that cow in the mornings before he went off to school and in the evenings when he got home. It wasn't his favorite chore. He said he used to daydream that he'd come home from school and she'd already be milked—but it never happened. He did become an expert at milking and to this day he remembers how good it was to have fresh buttermilk and cornbread. That is one of his most favorite comfort foods in the world—he just chops up some cornbread, dunks it into a glass of cold buttermilk, and eats it with a spoon.

My mom grew up around cows, too, and my grandma Cora would make delicious clotted cream from some of the milk. My grandpa always had to have something sweet after a meal, so oftentimes she'd turn the leftover biscuits from the morning into a dessert by splitting them, filling them with fresh clotted cream and sugar, then baking them in the oven until they caramelized like crème brûlée.

Spicy Cornbread Muffins
with Fresh White Corn

This bread is great on its own and also serves as the base for Faith's Herbed Cornbread Dressing with White Corn and Scallions (page 176). Most often we'd bake our cornbread in a cast-iron skillet, which creates a nice crust all around, but nowadays I bake my cornbread in muffin tins: It bakes up faster and it's also nice to pass a basketful when you're entertaining.

MAKES 12 MUFFINS

> 2 cups yellow cornmeal, plus additional for the pan
> 1 cup all-purpose flour
> 1 teaspoon sugar
> 1 tablespoon baking powder
> 1 teaspoon salt
> 1 large egg
> 1¼ cups milk
> 1 cup sweet white or yellow corn kernels
>   (from 1 ear of corn, or thawed if frozen)
> 2 tablespoons chopped pickled jalapeño
> 3 tablespoons vegetable oil

1. Preheat the oven to 400 degrees F.
2. In a large bowl, whisk together the cornmeal, flour, sugar, baking powder, and salt. In another bowl, beat the egg with the milk. Pour the wet ingredients over the dry ingredients and mix until just smooth. Fold the mixture a few more times for a lighter cornbread. Fold in the corn and jalapeño.
3. Divide the vegetable oil or bacon drippings among the cups of a dozen-count muffin tin. Place the tin in the oven for 5 minutes. Carefully remove the tin from the oven, swirl the oil onto the sides of the cups, and sprinkle in cornmeal to coat the bottoms. Scrape in the batter and use a rubber spatula to smooth the oil that rises on the sides over the top of the batter (this helps form a nice crust).
4. Bake until the tops are golden brown and spring back when lightly pressed, about 18 minutes. Let the muffins cool for 10 minutes, then turn onto a plate and serve warm.

Parmesan-Herb Cornbread Muffins

My mom adds things like pepper or crumbled bacon to her basic cornbread to give it different tastes. I take my mom's idea even further, adding fresh herbs, Parmesan cheese, paprika, and garlic to the mix. Many Southerners use bacon drippings to coat the baking pan, but I am "heart smart" and typically use vegetable oil instead. Melted butter is nice if you feel decadent.

MAKES 24 MUFFINS

¼ cup vegetable oil, melted bacon drippings, or melted butter

1½ cups all-purpose flour

1 cup yellow cornmeal, plus additional for the muffin tins

1 tablespoon chopped fresh basil, or 1 teaspoon dried

1 tablespoon chopped fresh oregano, or 1 teaspoon dried

2 teaspoons baking powder

1 teaspoon baking soda

1 teaspoon salt

1 teaspoon sugar

½ teaspoon paprika

½ teaspoon black pepper

2 cups milk

2 large eggs

½ cup grated Parmesan cheese

1 garlic clove, minced or passed through a garlic press

1. Preheat the oven to 375 degrees F. Position a rack in the middle of the oven. Fill each cup of 2 dozen-count muffin tins with ½ teaspoon vegetable oil, drippings, or butter. About 3 minutes before you are ready to bake, place the muffin tins in the oven to warm the oil.
2. In a mixing bowl, mix together the flour, cornmeal, basil, oregano, baking powder, baking soda, salt, sugar, paprika, and black pepper.

3. In a separate mixing bowl, beat together the milk, eggs, cheese, and garlic. Add the wet ingredients to the dry ingredients and mix gently until just combined.

4. Sprinkle a pinch of cornmeal into each warmed and oiled muffin cup. Fill each cup half full of batter and bake for about 15 minutes, until the tops are golden and spring back when lightly pressed. Let cool for 10 minutes then turn out onto a plate and serve warm.

My love affair with good food started early. I relished
(and evidently rolled in) every bite!

Peach-Pecan Bran Muffins

I hold all peaches to the standard set by my grandma Cora's peach tree. Not many have met the challenge, but when I do find really good, really juicy ripe peaches, I use them in everything I can. Pureeing a couple of the peaches adds moisture to these muffins and packs a delicious peachy taste into every bite.

MAKES 24 MUFFINS

1 cup wheat bran

2 cups all-purpose flour

2½ teaspoons baking soda

1 teaspoon ground cinnamon

½ teaspoon salt

3 ripe peaches, peeled (see page 251)

½ cup cane syrup (see Sources, page 267)

⅓ cup packed brown sugar

¼ cup honey

¼ cup vegetable oil

2 large eggs

1 cup chopped toasted pecans (see page 244)

1. Preheat the oven to 400 degrees F. Grease two dozen-count muffin tins.
2. In a small bowl, combine the wheat bran with ⅔ cup boiling water. Let stand for 15 minutes.
3. In another bowl, stir together the flour, baking soda, cinnamon, and salt.
4. In a food processor or blender, puree two of the peaches. Slice the third peach into small chunks.
5. In another bowl, whisk together the peach puree, syrup, sugar, honey, oil, and eggs. Stir in the wheat bran. Pour the wet mixture into the dry mixture and stir gently until just combined. Stir in the peach chunks and ½ cup of the chopped pecans. Do not overmix.
6. Spoon the batter into the muffin tins and sprinkle the tops with the remaining ½ cup chopped pecans. Bake for about 12 minutes, until the tops are browned and spring

back when gently pressed. Let cool for 10 minutes, then turn out onto a plate and serve warm or at room temperature. The muffins will keep for up to 3 days, stored in the refrigerator in a covered container.

Grandma Cora's peach tree gave up
the essential ingredient for her
renowned cobbler (page 218).

Mom's Banana-Walnut Bread

When I was growing up, banana cake was my dad's favorite, but now that we all try to eat healthier, mom has started to adjust her recipes accordingly. When she does make a cake, she'll make it smaller, or she'll make this banana bread instead. This bread is not sweet or heavy, so it's great for dessert, breakfast, or a mid-afternoon snack.

❧ *Mom Says:* Very ripe bananas with dark spotted skins are the best for baking and make the bread moist and delicious. If you have more overripe bananas than you know what to do with, freeze them in a plastic freezer bag until you are ready to make the next banana bread. Just defrost before using them.

MAKES 2 LOAVES

> 1 cup vegetable oil, plus additional for the pans
> 1 cup self-rising flour (see Note, page 192), plus additional for the pans
> 4 very ripe bananas
> 1 cup granulated sugar
> 1 cup packed light brown sugar
> 4 large eggs, beaten
> ¼ cup buttermilk
> 2 cups whole-wheat flour
> 1 teaspoon baking soda
> 1 teaspoon ground cinnamon
> ½ teaspoon salt
> 1 cup chopped toasted walnuts (see page 244)

1. Preheat the oven to 350 degrees F. Grease two 9-inch loaf pans and lightly dust them with flour.
2. Place the bananas in a large bowl and mash them well with a fork. Beat in the granulated sugar, brown sugar, oil, eggs, and buttermilk.
3. Add the whole-wheat flour, self-rising flour, baking soda, cinnamon, and salt to the banana mixture and stir to combine. Fold in the walnuts and divide the mixture evenly between the two pans.

4. Bake until the tops are golden brown and a toothpick inserted into the center of each loaf comes out almost clean, 45 to 50 minutes. Let cool for 10 minutes on a wire rack before removing the breads from the pans, then cool the loaves completely on the rack. Once cool, the loaves (or just one) can be frozen, sealed tightly in a plastic freezer bag, for up to 1 month. Defrost before serving.

CHOCOLATE COFFEE

My grandparents favored a local dark-roasted coffee, and they would let me have a little in my milk to make coffee milk when I was small. But I never became a coffee drinker until years later, when I moved out to L.A. I had a lot of unfinished projects to do one day, so I decided to try one of those iced blended mochas that's like a coffee smoothie. When I came home, I was able to finish everything. I was twenty-five at the time, and had no idea about the powers of caffeine! Since then, I've been in the habit of having a cup of chocolate coffee midmorning. To make it, I melt a square of semisweet chocolate or about 1 tablespoon of chocolate chips in half a cup of milk in the microwave. Then pour the coffee in and stir.

Peaches-n-Creamy Shake

When I have to leave the house early, I usually don't want breakfast first thing, and on hot summer days I definitely don't feel like chewing anything. Instead, I crave cold liquids, so I often whip up a shake to take on the road. I freeze fruit when it's too ripe to eat and usually make my shakes with frozen fruit, which makes them cold but doesn't give you that too-cold-frozen-head-rush you sometimes get with smoothies. If I don't have frozen fruit, I use just enough ice to get the shake chilly, not watery.

MAKES 3½ CUPS, SERVING 2

> 1 cup ice (only if using fresh peaches)
> 1 cup milk
> ½ cup nonfat vanilla yogurt
> 2 small peaches, fresh or frozen, peeled (see page 251) and cut into chunks
> 2 tablespoons honey
> 1 tablespoon protein powder, optional
> 1 teaspoon ground cinnamon

Put all the ingredients into a blender and blend until smooth and creamy. Serve immediately.

Blueberry Brain Shake

Someone recently told me that blueberries are good for your brain. I'm not sure of the scientific evidence, but I drink this on workday mornings and it seems to help me with the massive amount of dialogue I have to memorize. And the cold, creamy drink, full of berries, vanilla yogurt, and some banana, tastes great.

MAKES 4½ CUPS, SERVING 2 TO 3

> 1 pint blueberries, fresh or frozen
> 1 banana
> 1 to 2 cups ice, if using fresh blueberries
> 1 cup milk
> 1 cup berry juice, such as cranberry or blueberry-blackberry
> ½ cup vanilla nonfat yogurt
> 1 to 2 tablespoons protein powder, optional

Put all the ingredients into a blender and blend until smooth and creamy. Serve immediately.

Fresh Mint Iced Tea

In the South, you usually get your iced tea sweet. But I don't like my tea too sweet anymore and when I do have sweet tea, I have it with mint. Mint grows like a weed in my garden, so I'm always trying to find things to do with it.

Growing up, we always made our tea strong and added sugar while it was hot so the sugar dissolved. In restaurants in other parts of the country, they'll give you bags of granulated sugar, and I just can't stand it! All that sugar just floats around near the bottom of the glass. At my house, I make a simple sugar syrup and set it out in a little pitcher, so people can add it to their tea to taste.

SERVES 4

> ¾ cup sugar
> ⅓ cup chopped fresh mint, plus additional sprigs for garnish
> 6 regular tea bags
> Ice cubes

1. Bring 8 cups water to a boil.
2. Measure the sugar into a small jar with a lid. Place the mint and tea bags in a large heat resistant pitcher.
3. Pour ½ cup of the boiling water into the sugar and stir to dissolve (the sugar syrup can be made a month ahead and stored in the refrigerator). Pour the remaining water over the mint and tea bags. Steep for 8 to 10 minutes, then strain out the tea bags and mint. (The tea will keep for 3 days, refrigerated.) If the tea is too strong, add water.
4. Pour the tea over glasses of ice and sweeten to taste with the sugar syrup. Serve with a sprig of fresh mint in each glass.

CHAPTER 9

Desserts

Big-Time Brownies

Moving from Louisiana to New York at age seventeen to start my modeling career was quite a culture shock. I knew no one! But that wasn't as much of a big deal as the fact that I missed my mother's food. And I lived in a hotel, so I couldn't cook for myself.

My mother decided that if she couldn't feed her daughter at home, she would send homemade food to her, which began her obsession with creating the perfect brownie because brownies are perfect for mailing. Each month she'd go into her "laboratory" and measure, sift, mix, and bake up batches of the chocolaty goodies, then ship them off to New York.

I would call her up the day they arrived. The box would be sitting opened in my lap. "Aaaah, they're so great," I would say, both cheeks stuffed full.

Little did my mother know that her brownies would be not only my main food source for the next week, but also that of some starving actress and model friends. Without a doubt these are the best, most sustaining, brownies ever.

⸙ *Mom Says:* This is one of the many bar cookie recipes I concocted when
Faith first went to New York. I found that using a single saucepan worked well
and went fast so that I could make several kinds of bars in a short time. That way
I could get them to UPS in the afternoon, do a two-day ship, and they would still
be good when they arrived. If you love really dark chocolate, you can melt 1 ounce
unsweetened and 2 ounces bittersweet chocolate with the butter.

MAKES 2 DOZEN LITTLE BROWNIES

1 cup (2 sticks) unsalted butter, plus additional for the pan

1 cup granulated sugar

1 cup packed light brown sugar

½ cup unsweetened cocoa powder

2 teaspoons vanilla extract

¼ teaspoon ground cinnamon

¼ teaspoon salt

3 large eggs

1½ cups all-purpose flour

1 cup chopped toasted pecans (see page 244)

1. Preheat the oven to 350 degrees F. Grease a 9-by-13-inch baking pan.
2. In a 3-quart saucepan over low heat, melt the butter. Turn off the heat and add the sugars, cocoa, vanilla, cinnamon, and salt, mixing well with a wooden spoon. Mix in the eggs one at a time. Gradually add the flour, stirring until smooth. Stir in the pecans.
3. Spread the batter evenly in the pan and bake for 22 to 25 minutes for moist, fudgy brownies or 28 to 30 minutes for drier, cakier ones. Allow the brownies to cool in the pan for 15 to 20 minutes before cutting them into 2-inch squares—if you can wait that long! These brownies will keep, well wrapped, for up to 1 week.

Buttermilk Brownies

In our family you would never buy a brownie. Those wrapped squares you see in stores seem like sacrilege. Although naturally I prefer fudgy brownies, these soft, cakey ones are an exception. The buttermilk gives them a slight tang, and the icing is rich and creamy. Take care not to overcook the icing, though, or it will crystallize.

MAKES 2 DOZEN LITTLE BROWNIES

Brownies

    Unsalted butter, for the pan
    2 large eggs
    ½ cup vegetable oil
    ⅓ cup buttermilk
    1½ cups sugar
    ⅓ cup unsweetened cocoa powder
    1½ cups all-purpose flour
    ½ teaspoon baking soda
    ½ teaspoon salt
    1 teaspoon vanilla extract

1. Preheat the oven to 350 degrees F. Grease a 9-by-13-inch baking pan.
2. In a saucepan, whisk together the eggs, oil, and buttermilk. Whisk in the sugar, then heat the mixture over medium-low heat, stirring with a wooden spoon, until the sugar dissolves (do not let the mixture come to a boil). Remove from the heat.
3. In a small bowl, whisk the cocoa with ½ cup water until smooth. Stir the cocoa mixture into the saucepan. Beat in the flour, baking soda, salt, and vanilla until smooth.
4. Pour the batter into the prepared pan and bake until the center is just firm when lightly pressed, 25 to 30 minutes. Ice the brownies while they are still hot.

Icing

> 8 tablespoons (1 stick) unsalted butter
> ⅓ cup unsweetened cocoa powder
> ¼ cup buttermilk
> ½ teaspoon salt
> 2½ cups confectioners' sugar
> 1 teaspoon vanilla extract
> 1 cup chopped toasted nuts of choice (see page 244)

1. Place the butter in a saucepan and melt it over medium heat. Whisk in the cocoa, buttermilk, and salt until smooth. Beat in the sugar and stir until thoroughly incorporated. Remove the pan from the heat and stir in the vanilla. If the brownies are still baking, set the icing aside.

2. Give the icing a stir before spreading it over the hot brownies. Smooth the icing with a spatula and top it with the nuts. Let the brownies cool for at least 30 minutes before cutting them into 2-inch squares. These brownies will keep, well wrapped, for up to 1 week.

Chocolate Chip–Coconut Brownies

Another of my mother's winners, these special brownies make good use of coconut, a traditional Southern ingredient.

✧ *Mom Says:* For a gooey center almost like fudge, underbake these by a few minutes.

MAKES 2 DOZEN LITTLE BROWNIES

> 8 tablespoons (1 stick) unsalted butter, plus additional for the pan
> ⅓ cup unsweetened cocoa powder
> 1 teaspoon vanilla extract
> 1 cup self-rising flour (see Note, page 192)
> 1 cup sweetened coconut flakes
> 1 cup granulated sugar
> ½ packed cup light brown sugar
> ¼ teaspoon salt
> 2 large eggs, beaten
> 1 cup chocolate chips

1. Preheat the oven to 325 degrees F. Grease a 9-by-13-inch pan.
2. In a small bowl, combine the cocoa with ½ cup water. Add the vanilla and stir until smooth. In another bowl, stir together the flour and coconut.
3. In a saucepan over medium heat, melt the butter. Take the pan off the heat and stir in the sugars and salt. Add the eggs and mix until combined. Gradually stir in the flour-coconut mixture until well blended. Stir in the cocoa mixture.
4. Spread the batter evenly in the baking pan and sprinkle the chocolate chips over the top. Bake until the center begins to firm and a toothpick inserted in the center comes out clean, about 25 minutes. Let the brownies cool in the pan before cutting into 2-inch squares. These brownies will keep, well wrapped, for up to 1 week.

Faith's Peach and
Granola Crumble

For a long time I wouldn't bother with dessert when I had company, and mom just couldn't believe it. She thinks it's bad manners to have people over and not offer them something sweet. When I do make dessert, it's usually something on the lighter side, like this crumble. It's mostly peaches with a thin layer of crunchy granola on top, so it appeals to my health conscious Los Angeles friends. It's easy to make and is always a big hit. Serve it with vanilla frozen yogurt if you like.

SERVES 8

8 medium peaches (2 pounds), peeled (see page 251) and sliced

2 tablespoons granulated sugar

1 teaspoon ground cinnamon

$\frac{1}{2}$ teaspoon grated nutmeg

$1\frac{1}{2}$ cups Maple-Pecan Granola (page 188) or your favorite
    purchased nut granola

$\frac{3}{4}$ cup all-purpose flour

$\frac{3}{4}$ cup packed light brown sugar

4 tablespoons ($\frac{1}{2}$ stick) unsalted butter, melted

1. Preheat the oven to 350 degrees F.
2. In an 8-inch square (or similar sized) baking dish, toss together the peaches, sugar, cinnamon, and nutmeg.
3. In a bowl, combine the granola, flour, and brown sugar. Pour on the melted butter and mix until crumbly.
4. Sprinkle the crumble evenly over the peaches and bake for about 40 minutes, until browned on top and bubbly. Serve warm. This crumble will keep, covered and refrigerated, for up to 2 days, but is best eaten on the day it's made.

Cora's Peach Cobbler

My grandma Cora was the "chief" in the family when it came to cooking. She could make just about anything taste good. But it was her summertime peach cobbler that made my heart sing. On hot days, her cobbler topped with homemade vanilla ice cream sent me into orbit. I still remember how she giggled when I praised her special touch with this simple dish.

One sweltering weekend, while living in the San Fernando Valley in Los Angeles, I decided I had to have Cora's cobbler. So I called her for the recipe.

"Well, I don't know." Cora giggled. "I just cut up my peaches, then put a cuppa sugar and . . ."

Now, you would have to know Cora to realize that what she meant wasn't really a cup at all. It was an old coffee cup with the handle broken off that she used as a sugar scoop. It also came in handy as a flour scoop. I say, whatever works.

This is her recipe. It makes a tender, buttery, cakelike cobbler, as opposed to my mother's blackberry cobbler (page 220), which is topped with flaky biscuits. Both are delicious, so don't ask which I like better!

⚡ **Mom Says:** My mother made only peach cobbler, but you can also use nectarines or plums and/or berries. And she never used more than 4 cups of fruit at a time. She put her peaches up in quart-sized jars, in sugary syrup, all ready for baking. You didn't want to use more than one jar at a time since they had to last all winter—there was no going to the store for more!

SERVES 8

1¼ cups plus 1 tablespoon sugar
1 teaspoon ground cinnamon
1 tablespoon cornstarch
10 medium peaches (2½ pounds), peeled (see page 251) and sliced
1 cup all-purpose flour
1 teaspoon baking powder
Pinch of salt
¾ cup milk
8 tablespoons (1 stick) unsalted butter, cut into pieces

1. Preheat the oven to 350 degrees F. To make cinnamon sugar, combine the 1 tablespoon sugar with the cinnamon. Set aside.
2. In a saucepan over medium heat, stir together ¾ cup of the sugar, ¾ cup water, and the cornstarch. Bring to a boil and simmer until the mixture is clear, about 2 minutes. Add the fruit and bring the mixture back to a boil, then immediately pour it into a 9-by-12-inch baking dish.
3. In a bowl, whisk together the remaining ½ cup sugar with the flour, baking powder, and salt. Add the milk and stir until fairly smooth (this mixture is like pancake batter—better to leave a few small lumps than to overmix).
4. Drizzle the batter evenly over the fruit. Dot the butter over the batter, then sprinkle with the cinnamon sugar.
5. Bake the cobbler until the topping is crisp, golden brown, and cakelike in texture, about 1 hour. Let it cool in the pan before serving. This cobbler will keep, covered and refrigerated, for up to 2 days, but it's best served the day it's made.

Mom's Blackberry Cobbler with Biscuit Topping

There are different schools of thought when it comes to cobbler toppings. Some, like my grandma Cora's, are soft and cakey. Others, made with a biscuit topping, are crisp on top and juicy underneath. That's how my mom always makes her cobblers. I like it both ways—actually, I like cobbler almost any way as long as it has plenty of ripe fruit and a scoop of ice cream on top.

This is an adaptable recipe, so you can use it with most kinds of fruits, such as peaches, plums, and other berries.

Mom Says: My mom never made her blackberry cobbler with cinnamon. I decided to try it one day and have used it ever since. My husband, Charles, loves to pick blackberries because he enjoys my blackberry cobbler so much.

SERVES 8

6 cups ripe blackberries, picked over
1 cup plus 2 tablespoons sugar
2 tablespoons cornstarch
Pinch of salt
1 cup self-rising flour (see Note, page 192)
4 tablespoons (½ stick) unsalted chilled butter, cut into pieces
7 tablespoons half-and-half
½ teaspoon ground cinnamon, optional
2 tablespoons unsalted butter, melted, optional

1. Place the berries in a saucepan and add 1 to 1½ cups of water, to cover. Add the 1 cup sugar, the cornstarch, and salt and bring to a boil. Reduce the heat to low and simmer until the juice thickens, 5 minutes or so. Set the filling aside while you make the biscuits, or let cool, cover, and refrigerate for up to 2 days, until ready to use.
2. To prepare the biscuit topping, place the flour and butter in a food processor and pulse for a few seconds. Alternatively, cut the butter into the flour with two knives. Gradually add the half-and-half a couple of tablespoons at a time, pulsing or stirring

briefly after each addition. Pulse or stir until the mixture just comes together. Do not overmix. Place the mixture on a large piece of plastic wrap, pat it into a disc, then wrap it well and refrigerate for at least 1 hour and up to 2 days.

3. Preheat the oven to 350 degrees F.
4. Roll the biscuit dough out to a ¼-inch thickness between sheets of plastic wrap. Sprinkle the dough with the remaining 2 tablespoons sugar and the cinnamon.
5. Use a cookie cutter or the rim of a glass to cut out round biscuits, saving the excess dough. Crumble the excess dough into the bottom of a 9-by-12-inch baking pan. Pour the berry mixture into the pan, then arrange the biscuits on top. Drizzle the melted butter over the biscuits if desired, and bake until the biscuits are golden brown, about 30 minutes. Serve the cobbler warm with ice cream or whipped cream.

I made mom's blackberry cobbler for a New Year's Day gathering with some friends recently; it was a huge hit.

The Best Pie Crust

When my mom makes dough for pie crusts, she'll make enough for at least two or three crusts, and then she'll make two or three pies at a time. I usually make one at a time, even though mom says it's a waste of effort. I understand her argument: if you've got a dinner party and everyone has a slice, then the pie's gone, so if you want another slice the next day, you don't have it. But in my world, I like it to be gone so I don't eat all the leftovers myself!

✦ *Mom Says:* I have made this crust with shortening and with butter. The shortening crust is flakier, while the butter crust has a better taste. For the best of both worlds, try ½ cup unsalted butter and ½ cup shortening. And, if for some reason you don't want to make so many pies at once, you can freeze portions of the dough for up to 3 months.

MAKES THREE 9-INCH SINGLE CRUSTS

> 3 cups all-purpose flour
> 1½ teaspoons salt
> 1 cup (2 sticks) unsalted butter or solid vegetable shortening
> 1 large egg
> 1 teaspoon white vinegar

1. Put the flour and salt in a bowl or food processor. Add the butter and cut it in with a pastry cutter or two knives or pulse it in the food processor until it resembles oatmeal. Do not over mix.

2. In a small bowl, beat together ¼ cup cold water, the egg, and vinegar. Pour this over the flour mixture and mix it in with a fork or pulse a few times until just combined. If the dough does not come together, add 1 or 2 more tablespoons cold water. Divide the dough into three parts. Refrigerate the dough for about 15 minutes before rolling out or wrap tightly and refrigerate for up to 2 days or freeze for up to 3 months. Defrost for several hours or overnight before using.

3. If your recipe calls for a prebaked pie crust, preheat the oven to 375 degrees F. On a lightly floured surface, roll out one-third of the dough to an 11-inch round. Transfer

the dough to a 9-inch pie pan and trim the edges. Prick the bottom all over with a fork. Line the pie shell with foil, then fill it with pie weights or dried beans.

4. Bake for 15 minutes. Remove the weights and foil, then bake the crust for another 10 minutes until just golden. Let cool completely before filling. Prebaked pie crusts will keep, well wrapped, for up to 1 day stored at room temperature, but they're best used the day they're baked.

Showing off the first pie I baked for my husband, Campion.

Apple Crunch Pie

My mother doesn't usually make covered pies. For the top, she generally just sprinkles on crumble. I add pecans to the topping for extra crunch. If you don't feel like rolling out pie dough, just turn this into a crunchy apple crumble dessert by baking the fruit in an oblong baking dish or in little individual oven-safe dishes, with topping sprinkled over it.

MAKES ONE 9-INCH PIE, SERVING 8

> ⅓ recipe Best Pie Crust dough (page 222), or a purchased
>   9-inch refrigerated pie crust
> 6 medium or 4 large tart apples, such as Granny Smith, peeled and
>   thinly sliced (about 6 cups)
> 1¼ cups all-purpose flour
> ½ cup packed brown sugar
> ¼ cup plus 1 tablespoon granulated sugar
> 1½ teaspoons ground cinnamon
> ¾ teaspoon salt
> ¼ teaspoon grated nutmeg
> ¼ teaspoon ground cloves
> 8 tablespoons (1 stick) unsalted butter
> 1 cup chopped toasted pecans (see page 244), optional

1. Preheat the oven to 450 degrees F. On a lightly floured surface, roll out the pie dough to an 11-inch round and place it in a 9-inch pie pan. Trim the edges.
2. Put the apple slices in a large bowl with ¼ cup of the flour, ¼ cup of the brown sugar, the 1 tablespoon granulated sugar, 1 teaspoon of the cinnamon, ¼ teaspoon of the salt, the nutmeg, and cloves. Toss to coat the apples well. Pile the filling into the pie shell. Cut 2 tablespoons of the butter in pieces and dot it over the apples.
3. Put the remaining cup flour, ¼ cup brown sugar, ¼ cup granulated sugar, ½ teaspoon cinnamon, and ½ teaspoon salt into a bowl. Add the remaining 6 tablespoons butter and cut it in with a pastry cutter or two knives until the mixture resembles coarse crumbs. Mix in the pecans, if desired, and crumble the topping over the pie. The pie will be high—pat the topping a little so it adheres.

4. Bake the pie for 15 minutes, then reduce the heat to 350 degrees F and bake for about 30 more minutes, until the filling is bubbling and the apples are tender. Let the pie cool on a wire rack for at least 30 minutes before serving. This pie will keep, covered and refrigerated, for up to 2 days, but is best served on the day it's made.

From apple crunch (page 224) to blueberry (page 226),
chocolate chip–pecan (page 234) to classic vanilla cream (page 230),
my mom makes the best pie crust (page 222).

Pint-Sized Blueberry Pie

This is the perfect pie to make when you don't want too much pie! It uses exactly one pint of blueberries, and fits in one of those disposable aluminum pie plates, so it is a very fast dessert to put together if you use purchased pie shells. If you use a regular pie plate, use the smallest you have—the 8- or 9-inch plates that actually measure only 7 inches across the bottom are best.

In my family, we put a crumb crust on top of apple pies, but blueberry pies always get a double crust. I suppose it's because apples tend to be more tart, whereas blueberries are already sweet, so we wouldn't want to add a sugary crumb topping. And berries are so juicy and bubble up so much, a top crust keeps them contained. My mother sometimes gets fancy and does a lattice crust on top, but usually she keeps the top crust simple with a couple of vent holes. I usually put little designs like stars or leaves on top made from extra dough. If you do this, wet the dough with a little milk so the decorations stick.

✣ *Mom Says:* Personally, I think that most blueberry pie recipes are too sweet. This one's the exception. It's just sweet enough.

MAKES ONE 8- TO 9-INCH PIE, SERVING 8

⅔ recipe Best Pie Crust dough (page 222), or
    2 purchased 9-inch refrigerated pie crusts
½ cup plus 1 teaspoon sugar
½ teaspoon ground cinnamon
⅓ cup cornstarch
1 tablespoon freshly squeezed lemon juice
¼ teaspoon salt
1 pint fresh blueberries, or 2 cups frozen (no need to thaw them first)
2 tablespoons unsalted butter, melted

1. Preheat the oven to 400 degrees F. Set a rack on the lowest shelf of the oven.
2. On a lightly floured surface, roll out half the pie dough to a 10-inch round and place it in an 8-inch pie pan. Trim the edges. Roll out the other half to an 11-inch round for the top crust and set it aside.

3. To make the cinnamon sugar, combine the 1 teaspoon sugar with ¼ teaspoon of the cinnamon. Set aside.

4. In a saucepan over medium heat, combine ½ cup water, the remaining ½ cup sugar, the cornstarch, lemon juice, and salt. Stir until dissolved. Bring to a boil, stirring constantly, until the mixture thickens but does not turn clear, about 3 minutes.

5. Put the berries in the unbaked pie shell and pour the glaze over the top. Sprinkle the remaining ¼ teaspoon cinnamon over the berries and drizzle on 1 tablespoon of the melted butter. Cover with the top crust and crimp the edges to seal. Use a small knife to make several vent holes in the top. Brush the top with the remaining tablespoon melted butter and sprinkle with the cinnamon sugar.

6. Place the pie pan on a rimmed baking sheet (to prevent spills on the bottom of the oven) and bake for about 30 minutes, until the filling is bubbling. (If the crust begins to get too brown, cover it with foil and continue baking.) Transfer the pie to a cooling rack and let sit for 1 to 2 hours before serving so that the juice will not be too runny. This pie will keep, covered and refrigerated, for up to 2 days, but is best served on the day it's made.

Fresh Strawberry Pie with Whipped Cream

In Louisiana, when the strawberries start coming in early spring, you know it's time to make fresh strawberry pies. Mom would bring home big trays of berries and we never just ate them—they were for pies. Strawberry pies were a special treat when we had guests, and I really looked forward to them. They're not too sweet—if you make the pie too sugary and saucy, it defeats the purpose of using real fresh fruit.

⚜ *Mom Says:* I sometimes leave the cooked strawberries in my glaze, but Faith prefers it strained. This recipe can easily be doubled to make two pies, but I have found that these pies do not keep well for over a day or two because the crust gets soggy. So make only what you need or share one with a neighbor.

MAKES ONE 9-INCH PIE, SERVING 8

Crust

> 1 cup all-purpose flour
> 2 tablespoons sugar
> ¼ teaspoon salt
> 8 tablespoons (1 stick) unsalted butter, cut into pieces
> 1 egg white, beaten

1. In a food processor combine the flour, sugar, and salt and pulse to combine. Add the butter and pulse until the mixture resembles cornmeal. Alternatively, cut the butter into the dry ingredients using a pastry blender or two knives. Add 1 tablespoon cold water and pulse briefly until just combined. Gather the dough into a ball, wrap it in plastic, and let rest for 30 minutes.
2. Press the dough evenly into a 9-inch pie pan. Line it with foil and place in the freezer for 30 minutes or up to 3 months. Make sure to wrap it in plastic if you plan to freeze it for more than 4 hours.
3. When you're ready to make the pie, preheat the oven to 375 degrees F.
4. Place dried beans or pie weights in an even layer over the foil and bake for 15 minutes. Remove the weights and foil and brush the entire surface of the crust with

beaten egg white (to seal the crust so it doesn't get too soggy once you add the filling), then return to the oven and bake for an additional 10 minutes until lightly golden. Let it cool to room temperature on a wire rack. The crust can be kept, covered, for up to 1 day stored at room temperature.

Glaze, Filling, and Topping
    2 pounds (4 pints) fresh strawberries, hulled
    ½ cup sugar
    2 tablespoons cornstarch
    1 cup heavy cream
    1 tablespoon honey

1. Set aside a few of the biggest and prettiest strawberries for the top, then slice enough of the smaller, less perfect strawberries to equal 1 cup.
2. Place the sliced berries and 1 cup water in a saucepan and let simmer, covered, for 15 to 20 minutes, until most of the color has cooked out of the berries. Strain the juice into a bowl, pressing down gently on the strawberries, then discard them.
3. Pour all but 2 tablespoons of the juice back into the pan and add the sugar. Whisk the cornstarch into the reserved juice in the bowl, then add that to the pan. Cook, stirring frequently, over medium heat for about 10 minutes, until the mixture thickens. Set aside to cool completely.
4. While the glaze is cooling, arrange the least perfect whole berries in a single layer, trimmed end down, in the cooled crust. Ladle the cooled glaze over the berries and refrigerate until set, at least 1 hour and no longer than 1 day.
5. Chill a metal mixing bowl in the freezer for at least 15 minutes. Just before serving, remove the bowl from the freezer and whip the cream until soft peaks form. Quickly whip in the honey. Top the pie with the sweetened cream. Slice the reserved large and pretty strawberries and garnish the top of the pie with them. Alternatively, serve the pie with the whipped cream and sliced berries on the side.

Classic Vanilla Cream Pie with Variations

This master recipe for vanilla cream pie can become any variety of cream pie with the addition of a few flavorings. When mom makes cream pies, she usually does a big recipe of vanilla cream filling, then splits it up and flavors half with chocolate and half with coconut (my personal favorite) or half with banana and half with pineapple—I won't turn any of them down. My mother really knows how to make cream pies the right way. My big, beautiful meringues look like hers, but they sometimes creep away from the edges. The secret is, when you put the hot cream filling inside the shell, you want to get the meringue on as quickly as possible so that it starts to cook before it hits the oven. It's all in the timing. If you don't get it quite right, don't worry—the pie may not be as pretty, but it'll definitely taste as good.

Mom Says: Pie shells for cream pies should always be prebaked (see page 222) and thoroughly cooled before filling.

MAKES ONE 9-INCH PIE, SERVING 8

1/3 recipe Best Pie Crust (page 222), prebaked in a 9-inch pan and cooled, or a purchased 9-inch prebaked crust, such as a graham cracker crust

Vanilla Cream Filling

2/3 cup sugar
1/4 cup cornstarch
1/2 teaspoon salt
2 1/2 cups milk
3 large egg yolks, beaten (save the whites for the meringue)
2 tablespoons unsalted butter
2 teaspoons vanilla extract

1. Preheat the oven to 325 degrees F. In a saucepan, whisk together the sugar, cornstarch, and salt. Whisk in the milk. Place the pan over medium heat and cook, stir-

ring constantly and regulating the heat so that the mixture does not boil or scorch, until it is thick enough to coat the back of a spoon.

2. Ladle about 1 cup of the hot milk mixture into the yolks, whisking constantly, and mix well. Pour this mixture back into the saucepan, still whisking constantly. Bring to a simmer and cook, stirring constantly, regulating the heat so that the mixture keeps bubbling, for 5 minutes. Stir in the butter and vanilla and take the pan off the heat. Cover the filling to keep it warm while you prepare the meringue.

Meringue Topping
>   3 large egg whites, at room temperature
>   6 tablespoons confectioners' sugar
>   1/4 teaspoon cream of tartar
>   1 teaspoon vanilla extract

1. In the clean dry bowl of an electric mixer beat the egg whites on high until fluffy. Add the confectioners' sugar 1 tablespoon at a time, beating after each addition. Then add the cream of tartar and beat until the whites hold a stiff peak. Beat in the vanilla.
2. Pour the hot cream filling into the pie crust. Spoon the meringue onto the filling, starting with a border at the edge of the crust to ensure that the meringue is anchored to the crust all around. Bake until the meringue is lightly browned, 10 to 15 minutes. Let the pie cool thoroughly before serving. This pie will keep, covered and refrigerated, for up to 2 days, but is best served on the day it's made.

Banana Cream Pie

Follow the directions for Vanilla Cream Pie (page 230). Peel and slice 1 1/2 large or 2 small ripe bananas. Pour half the filling into the crust, then arrange half of the bananas in a single layer over the filling. Top with the remaining filling and a second layer of bananas. Top with meringue and bake as directed.

Coconut Cream Pie

Follow the directions for Vanilla Cream Pie (page 230), but reduce the vanilla to 1 teaspoon and add 1/4 teaspoon almond extract (or to taste). Stir 1 cup sweetened coconut flakes into the custard before pouring it into the pie shell.

Caramel Cream Pie

1. Follow the directions for Vanilla Cream Pie (page 230), but, in a small saucepan over medium heat, warm the milk only. Add the cornstarch and salt and whisk until combined. Set aside.
2. Place the sugar in a heavy saucepan, preferably with a light-colored interior, over medium-low heat. Heat the sugar, stirring occasionally so it melts evenly. Cook until the sugar is light brown, then immediately take the pan off the heat and pour in the hot milk mixture (stand back, the caramel may splatter). Whisk until smooth, then cook over medium heat until the mixture is thick enough to coat the back of a spoon. Proceed as for regular cream pie.

Coconut-Caramel Cream Pie

Follow the directions for Caramel Cream Pie (above), but stir ½ cup sweetened coconut flakes into the custard before pouring it into the pie shell.

Chocolate Cream Pie

Dissolve ⅓ cup unsweetened cocoa powder in ¼ cup hot water. Follow the directions for Vanilla Cream Pie (page 230), but increase the sugar to 1 cup and add the cocoa mixture to the milk mixture before cooking the custard. Reduce the vanilla to 1 teaspoon and add ¼ teaspoon almond extract (or to taste) and ¼ teaspoon ground cinnamon.

Chocolate-Coconut Cream Pie

Follow the directions for Chocolate Cream Pie (above), but stir 1 cup sweetened coconut flakes into the custard before pouring it into the pie shell.

Peachy Cream Pie

Follow the directions for Vanilla Cream Pie (page 230), but drain one 14-ounce can sliced peaches, reserving ½ cup of the juice to use in place of ½ cup of the milk. Reduce the vanilla extract to 1 teaspoon, add ¼ teaspoon cinnamon if desired, and fold the peach slices into the custard before pouring it into the pie shell.

Peanut Butter Cream Pie

Follow the directions for Vanilla Cream Pie (page 230), but substitute 1 cup light brown for the white sugar, stir in ½ cup crunchy (or smooth) peanut butter instead of the butter, and reduce the vanilla to 1 teaspoon.

Pineapple Cream Pie

Follow the directions for Vanilla Cream Pie (page 230), but drain one 15-ounce can of crushed pineapple, reserving ½ cup of the juice to use in place of ½ cup of the milk. Reduce the vanilla extract to 1 teaspoon and fold the pineapple into the custard before pouring it into the pie shell.

Pineapple-Coconut Cream Pie

Follow the directions for Pineapple Cream Pie (above), but stir ½ cup sweetened coconut flakes into the custard before pouring it into the pie shell.

Chocolate Chip–Pecan Pie

This is another recipe from mom, the queen pie maker in the family. The thing about all her pies, and this one in particular, is that she makes sure none of them is too sweet. The semi-sweet chocolate chips in this recipe definitely help cut the syrupy filling of pecan pie. She mixes in half the chocolate chips before baking, and then sprinkles the rest on top of the pie when it is halfway done, so that the pie is full of melted chocolate inside while the chips on the top remain intact. We serve this with whipped cream, ice cream, or frozen yogurt.

MAKES ONE 9-INCH PIE, SERVING 8

⅓ recipe Best Pie Crust dough (page 222), or a purchased
    9-inch refrigerated pie crust
1 cup light corn syrup
¼ cup packed light brown sugar
2 large eggs, beaten
2 tablespoons unsalted butter, melted
2 tablespoons all-purpose flour
1 teaspoon vanilla extract
½ teaspoon salt
1 cup coarsely chopped toasted pecans (see page 244)
1 cup semisweet chocolate chips
Whipped cream

1. Preheat the oven to 350 degrees F. On a floured surface, roll out the pie dough to an 11-inch round and place it in a 9-inch pie pan. Trim the edges.
2. Put the corn syrup, brown sugar, eggs, butter, flour, vanilla, and salt in a bowl and mix well. Add the pecans and ½ cup of the chocolate chips. Pour the mixture into the pie shell.
3. Bake for 30 minutes. Remove the pie from the oven and sprinkle the remaining chocolate chips evenly on top (if you add them sooner, the chips will fall to the bottom and cook into the mix). Return the pie to the oven and bake for 30 more minutes. The outside edges should be firm, while the inside will still be a little wobbly. The pie will fully set as it cools on a wire rack. Serve at room temperature. This pie will keep, covered, for up to 4 days, but is best served on the day it's made, topped with whipped cream.

Mini Maple Pecan Pies

My aunt Brenda came up with the idea of making mini pecan pies one Christmas and now I always make them around Christmastime. Making lots of tiny pies might seem painstaking but they're actually easy to turn out. Brenda uses a pat-in-the-pan cream cheese crust for hers, but I find that using the Best Pie Crust recipe with all butter is the most crisp. And I use maple syrup, which has a nice flavor, and as many nuts as possible. This recipe doubles or triples easily, so you can make mini pecan pies for everyone!

MAKES 12 MINI PIES

> ⅓ recipe Best Pie Crust dough (page 222), or a purchased
>   9-inch refrigerated pie crust
> 1 cup chopped toasted pecans (see page 244)
> ½ cup pure maple syrup
> 1 large egg, beaten
> 1 tablespoon unsalted butter, melted
> 1 teaspoon vanilla extract
> ½ teaspoon salt

1. Preheat the oven to 350 degrees F. On a lightly floured surface, roll out the pie dough to ⅛ inch thick and cut out 3-inch circles. Press the circles into a dozen-count muffin tin.
2. Put the pecans, maple syrup, egg, butter, vanilla, and salt into a bowl and mix well. Fill the muffin cups with the filling. Bake for 30 to 35 minutes, until set. Cool the pan slightly on a wire rack then pop the pies out of the muffin tins and let them cool completely on the rack. These pies can be kept, well wrapped, for up to 4 days, but are best served on the day they're made.

Heavenly Pineapple Pie

This pie immediately brings to mind my childhood. I was never a big sweets eater, even when I was little, but there was something about this pie that I really liked. It's cold, crunchy, refreshing, and soothing—heavenly, really.

MAKES ONE 9-INCH PIE, SERVING 8

1 (15-ounce) can crushed pineapple

2 tablespoons sugar

2 tablespoons cornstarch

$\frac{1}{8}$ teaspoon salt

1 large egg

$1\frac{1}{4}$ cups mini marshmallows

$\frac{1}{2}$ cup heavy cream

$\frac{1}{3}$ recipe Best Pie Crust (page 222), prebaked in a 9-inch pan and cooled, or a purchased 9-inch prebaked pie crust, such as a graham cracker crust

$\frac{1}{2}$ cup coarsely chopped toasted pecans (see page 244)

1. Place a sieve over a medium saucepan. Pour the crushed pineapple into the sieve and press down so that most of the juice drains into the saucepan. Set the pineapple aside.
2. Add the sugar, cornstarch, and salt to the saucepan and whisk until no lumps remain. Begin cooking on medium heat, stirring constantly, until thickened and smooth, 5 to 7 minutes.
3. In a small bowl, beat the egg. Add a little of the hot mixture, stirring, then transfer the egg mixture into the saucepan, stirring quickly. Cook, stirring, on medium heat, until thick, 3 to 5 minutes.
4. Add the marshmallows and stir until dissolved. Turn off the heat. Stir in the reserved pineapple and chill, covered, in the refrigerator for 1 hour, or up to 1 day.
5. Whip the cream to stiff peaks. Gently fold the cream into the chilled pineapple mixture, then turn into the pie shell. Chill the pie for at least 1 hour or up to 1 day. Just before serving it, sprinkle with the chopped pecans.

Old-Fashioned Coconut Pie

My aunt Brenda found this recipe among some of my grandma Cora's things. It was hand-written, which of course makes it especially precious. This particular pie needs no crust—it makes its own. It's actually somewhere between a pie and a cake, completely delicious, and easy to make.

MAKES ONE 9-INCH PIE, SERVING 8

> 8 tablespoons (1 stick) unsalted butter, melted, plus
>   additional for the pie plate
> 1¼ cups sugar
> 4 large eggs
> 1 teaspoon vanilla extract
> 2 cups packed sweetened coconut flakes
> ½ cup self-rising flour (see Note, page 192)

1. Preheat the oven to 325 degrees F. Grease a 10-inch pie plate.
2. In a large bowl, beat together the sugar, eggs, and vanilla extract. Add the coconut, butter, and flour and stir until well combined.
3. Transfer the mixture to the prepared pan and bake until the top is golden brown and the center is firm, 40 to 45 minutes. Let the pie cool on a wire rack before serving. This pie will keep, covered and refrigerated, for up to 3 days.

Fluffy Lemon Icebox Pie

I love refreshing, clean-tasting lemon pies and tarts and always order them in restaurants. My mom's pie is a big improvement on traditional lemon meringue pie, which has the lemon on the bottom and the meringue on top. Since she folds the fluffy egg whites into the lemon custard, everything gets blended into a mellow tartness that melts in your mouth. I especially love this pie with freshly whipped cream on top.

❧ *Mom Says:* Chilled "refrigerator" pies are great desserts to make when you're having company. I always have everything completely ready before guests arrive, so I swear by desserts I can make the night before. A graham cracker crust is nice here, and it makes this recipe even simpler.

MAKES ONE 9-INCH PIE, SERVING 8

1 (14-ounce) can sweetened condensed milk
3 large eggs, separated
4 tablespoons sugar
½ cup freshly squeezed lemon juice (from 2 to 3 lemons)
⅓ recipe Best Pie Crust (page 222), prebaked in a 9-inch pan and cooled, or a
    purchased 9-inch prebaked graham cracker crust
Whipped cream, optional

1. Preheat the oven to 325 degrees F. In a small bowl, whisk together the condensed milk and egg yolks until well combined.
2. In the clean dry bowl of an electric mixer, beat the egg whites until frothy. Add the sugar 1 tablespoon at a time and beat until the mixture holds firm peaks.
3. Working quickly, whisk the lemon juice into the milk and egg yolk mixture. Stir a little of the egg white mixture into the lemon mixture to lighten it. Fold the lemon mixture into the rest of the egg whites, until just combined.
4. Spoon the mixture into the pie shell and bake for 20 to 25 minutes, until the filling is set and the outside is golden and dry to the touch. Cool the pie on a wire rack for 1 hour, then refrigerate it for several hours or overnight. Serve it with whipped cream, if desired.

Grandma Cora's Applesauce Cake:
A Piece of Pat's Past

My mother, Cora, never followed a recipe exactly. When she made her applesauce layer cake, she would add more of each spice than was called for, and before baking the three layers of the cake she would spoon a big dollop of the mix into a tin pie plate and bake what she called a "try cake." This was probably something that was handed down from my grandmother. The cake would spread out in the pan and get puffy in the middle and crispy brown around the edges. She would take it out of the oven, immediately break off a warm piece, and taste it. Then she would give the rest to me and my little sister, Brenda; that was definitely the best part of making the cake. As we ate the "try cake," my mother would pick up one can of spice and then another and shake in a little more of each as she mumbled to herself that the batter needed a little more cinnamon or nutmeg or allspice or salt or even a little more soda, if it didn't rise as much as she thought it should. Then she would begin baking the layers of the real cake. They always turned out perfectly brown and never fell. When they came out of the oven she would cool them a bit, then turn each one face down on a clean towel to cool completely while she made the caramel icing.

And what an amazing icing it was—perfectly caramel brown and not sticky or runny—almost like smooth semisoft caramel fudge. When all the layers were assembled with the icing and walnuts, it was quite a sight to behold. She would make it several days before Christmas so that the flavors and moisture of the applesauce and raisins could fully penetrate the cake. This became the traditional fruitcake for our family, and we were not allowed to cut into it until Christmas Day.

Applesauce Cake with Caramel Icing

✧ *Mom Says:* Making this cake just looked so easy that I never thought to ask Mama to give me her recipe. I suppose it didn't occur to me that she wouldn't be around forever. When I was looking through her recipes after she passed on, I found this tiny little brown scrap from an old recipe book and on that scrap of paper was a recipe for applesauce cake. Thinking this might be *the* recipe, I put it away somewhere safe so that I would always be able to find it. Well, now I can't find it. But really, what does it matter? Mama didn't ever follow recipes anyway! What you'll find here is from my "brain file," the same place Mama kept most of her recipes.

MAKES ONE 9-INCH LAYER CAKE, SERVING 12

Layer Cakes

    1 cup (2 sticks) unsalted butter, softened, plus additional for the pans

    3 cups sifted all-purpose flour, plus additional for the pans

    2 teaspoons baking soda

    2 teaspoons ground cinnamon

    1 teaspoon grated nutmeg

    ¼ teaspoon ground cloves

    ¼ teaspoon ground allspice

    1 teaspoon salt

    2 cups sugar

    3 large eggs

    2½ cups unsweetened applesauce (one 23-ounce jar)

    2 teaspoons vanilla extract

    2 cups chopped raisins

    2 cups chopped toasted walnuts (see page 244)

1. Preheat the oven to 350 degrees F. Grease and flour three 9-inch cake pans.
2. Sift the flour, baking soda, cinnamon, nutmeg, cloves, allspice, and salt together in a large mixing bowl.
3. In another bowl, beat the sugar and butter together until fluffy, 3 to 5 minutes, then

add the eggs one at a time, beating well after each addition. Stir in the applesauce and vanilla, then begin mixing in the dry ingredients a little at a time until well combined. Fold in the raisins and walnuts.

4. Pour the batter into the prepared pans and bake for about 35 minutes, until the tops spring back when lightly pressed. Let the layers cool on a wire rack. The layers can be kept, well wrapped and refrigerated, for up to 2 days or frozen for up to 1 month.

Caramel Icing

 2½ cups sugar
 1½ cups heavy cream, plus additional if needed
 ½ teaspoon salt
 4 tablespoons (½ stick) unsalted butter
 ¼ teaspoon baking soda
 9 walnut halves, or ½ cup coarsely chopped toasted walnuts (see page 244)

1. Combine 1½ cups of the sugar, the cream, and salt in a heavy-bottomed saucepan. Bring to a simmer over medium-low heat, stirring until the sugar has dissolved.
2. Stir together the remaining 1 cup sugar and ¼ cup water in a small, heavy skillet (preferably one that has a pouring lip). Cook the sugar mixture over medium heat, without stirring, until it melts and turns an amber color, about 10 minutes.
3. Add the caramelized sugar to the simmering sugar and cream mixture a little at a time, stirring it up from the bottom (adding the caramelized sugar all at once will cause the mixture to boil over). Cook on medium heat until the mixture reaches the soft-ball stage (it will register 240 degrees F on a candy thermometer, and when a spoonful is dropped into a dish of very cold water, it will come together into a soft, malleable ball), about 10 minutes.
4. Take the mixture off the heat and stir in the butter and baking soda. Let cool slightly, or speed the process by placing the bottom of the saucepan in a pan of ice water and stirring constantly. Beat the mixture with a wooden spoon until it begins to lose gloss but is still easy to spread, 2 to 3 minutes.
5. Spread some of the icing thinly over a cooled cake layer, then stack another layer on top and repeat the process until all three layers are assembled. Spread icing over the top and around the sides of the cake, thinning the icing with a little more cream if it becomes too thick. Garnish the outside edge of the top of the cake with walnut halves or sprinkle the top with chopped walnuts. Wait to cut the cake until the moisture penetrates it (at least 1 day and up to 2 days) or it will tend to crumble. Store it at room temperature under a cake dome or lightly wrapped in plastic wrap for up to 4 days.

Grandma Cora's Spicy Fresh Pear Cake with Buttermilk Glaze

Here's another one of Grandma Cora's amazing cakes, though this one is plain and homey rather than fancy.

☙ *Mom Says:* My mother loved this recipe because we had plenty of pears on the farm. We would peel and chop pears, add some sugar, and freeze them in 3-cup packs to use later in cakes or pies. The sugar kept the fruit from toughening when you defrosted it.

This is a wonderful, moist cake that is even better the day after baking, when the juice from the pears penetrates the cake. But it's hard to wait because the cake smells heavenly when it's freshly baked. The glaze is a thin one and is brushed over the entire cake to seal in the moisture.

MAKES ONE 10-INCH BUNDT CAKE, SERVING 12

Cake

Unsalted butter, for the pan
3 cups all-purpose flour
2 cups sugar
2 teaspoons ground cinnamon
1 teaspoon baking soda
½ teaspoon salt
¼ teaspoon ground allspice, optional
1 cup vegetable oil
3 large eggs
2 teaspoons vanilla extract
3 large pears, peeled, cored, and chopped
1 cup chopped toasted pecans or walnuts (see page 244)

1. Preheat the oven to 350 degrees F. Grease a 10-inch Bundt pan.
2. In a medium bowl, whisk together the flour, sugar, cinnamon, baking soda, salt, and

allspice, if using. In another bowl, whisk together the oil, eggs, and vanilla. Add the wet ingredients to the dry and mix well. Fold in the pears and walnuts.

3. Pour the batter into the prepared pan and bake for about 1 hour and 10 minutes, until a skewer inserted into the cake comes out clean. Cool the cake on a wire rack for 10 minutes then turn it out of the pan and let it cool completely on the rack.

Glaze

½ cup confectioners' sugar
2 tablespoons buttermilk
½ teaspoon vanilla extract

While the cake is cooling, whisk together all the ingredients for the glaze. Brush the cooled cake all over with the glaze and allow it to set for at least an hour before cutting. This cake is best when made 1 day ahead. Store it at room temperature under a cake dome or lightly wrapped in plastic wrap for up to 4 days.

Fig Cake with Buttermilk Glaze

My grandma Cora would make preserves with figs that grew on the tree in her backyard and then use those preserves on biscuits or in this typical, very moist, Southern cake. You can use purchased preserves if you don't have time to make your own.

MAKES ONE 10-INCH BUNDT CAKE, SERVING 12

Cake

Unsalted butter, for the pan
2 cups all-purpose flour
1½ cups sugar
1 teaspoon baking soda
1 teaspoon salt
1 teaspoon ground cinnamon
1 teaspoon ground allspice
1 cup vegetable oil
1 cup buttermilk
3 large eggs
1 teaspoon vanilla extract
1 cup coarsely chopped toasted pecans (see Toasting Nuts)
1 cup coarsely chopped homemade fig preserves (page 265) or purchased preserves

TOASTING NUTS

Lightly toasting nuts in the oven brings out a rich, earthy flavor that enhances the dishes you use them in. To toast nuts, spread them in a single layer on a baking sheet and place them in a 350 degree F oven for 8 to 12 minutes, turning once or twice, until fragrant. Let cool slightly before using. Store toasted nuts in an airtight container for up to 6 months.

1. Preheat the oven to 350 degrees F. Grease a 10-inch Bundt pan.
2. In a large bowl, combine the flour, sugar, baking soda, salt, cinnamon, and allspice. In another bowl, whisk together the oil, buttermilk, eggs, and vanilla. Pour the wet ingredients into the dry ingredients and fold together. Fold in the nuts and preserves.
3. Transfer the mixture to the prepared pan and bake for 50 to 60 minutes, until a skewer inserted into the cake comes out clean. Cool the cake on a wire rack for 10 minutes then turn it out of the pan and let it cool completely on the rack.

Glaze

⅓ cup confectioners' sugar
3 tablespoons buttermilk

Whisk together the sugar and buttermilk. Brush all over the cooled cake to seal in the moisture. Let sit for 1 hour before cutting. This cake can be made 1 day ahead. Store at room temperature under a cake dome or lightly wrapped in plastic wrap.

Me, Ma Walker (my great-grandmother), and my sister, Devon.

Faith's Chocolate-Pecan
Layer Cake

Since chocolate cake was not particularly big in my family, I decided to make it a tradition of my own. This is now the official birthday cake at my house. I make this pecan version for my birthday on September 14 and then again with Campion's favorite peanut butter frosting (see Campion's Peanut Butter Frosting) for his birthday on November 12.

MAKES ONE 9-INCH LAYER CAKE, SERVING 12

Cake

> Unsalted butter, for the pans
> 1¾ cups all-purpose flour, plus additional for the pans
> 1½ cups sugar
> ¾ cup unsweetened cocoa powder
> 1½ teaspoons baking powder
> 1½ teaspoons baking soda
> 1 teaspoon salt
> 2 large eggs
> 1 cup milk
> ½ cup vegetable oil
> 2 teaspoons vanilla extract

1. Preheat the oven to 350 degrees F. Grease and flour two 9-inch cake pans. Bring 1 cup water to a boil.
2. In the bowl of an electric mixer fitted with the whisk attachment, stir together the flour, sugar, cocoa, baking powder, baking soda, and salt.
3. Add the eggs, milk, oil, and vanilla. Beat on medium speed for 2 minutes. Stir in the boiling water.
4. Pour the batter into the pans and bake for 30 to 35 minutes, or until a wooden toothpick comes out clean when inserted in the center. Let cool on wire racks for 10 minutes. Remove the cakes from the pans and let them cool completely before frosting. The layers can be kept, well wrapped and refrigerated, for up to 2 days, or frozen for up to 1 month.

Chocolate Frosting

    8 tablespoons (1 stick) unsalted butter, melted

    1 teaspoon vanilla extract

    $^2/_3$ cup unsweetened cocoa powder

    2 cups confectioners' sugar, plus additional if needed

    $^1/_3$ cup milk, plus additional if needed

    $1^1/_2$ cups chopped toasted pecans (see page 244)

1. Pour the butter and vanilla into the bowl of an electric mixer fitted with the whisk attachment and stir in the cocoa. Beat in half the confectioner's sugar, then half the milk, then repeat, beating on medium speed until smooth and light. Thin with additional milk or thicken with additional confectioners' sugar if necessary to get a spreadable consistency.

2. Spread about a third of the frosting on the first layer of cake and sprinkle with half of the chopped nuts. Place the second layer on top and frost the entire cake. Sprinkle the remaining chopped pecans on top of the cake. Store it at room temperature under a cake dome or lightly wrapped in plastic wrap for up to 3 days.

CAMPION'S PEANUT BUTTER FROSTING

    1 cup creamy peanut butter

    1 (8-ounce) package cream cheese

    1 cup confectioners' sugar

    1 teaspoon vanilla extract

    $1^1/_2$ cups roughly chopped roasted unsalted peanuts
       (see page 244)

Using an electric mixer, beat the peanut butter, cream cheese, sugar, and vanilla together. Spread about a third of the frosting on the first layer of cake, and sprinkle with half of the chopped nuts. Place the second layer on top and frost the entire cake. Sprinkle the remaining chopped peanuts on top of the cake.

Grandma Cora's Fluffy Catahoula Coconut Cake

There's nothing like offering someone a slice of homemade cake to make them feel loved. This showstopper was always a special-occasion layer cake at our house when I was growing up, the kind of thing my grandma Cora made for holidays. If you put this out on display during a meal, you can bet everyone will save room for dessert!

⚜ *Mom Says:* My sister, Brenda, and I remember that when we were little girls, Mama would make a fresh coconut cake and take it to the big family Christmas dinners at my dad's parents' house. It was a once-a-year occurrence, since we only got fresh coconuts at Christmastime. Once you got the coconut, you had to punch holes in two of the eyes to drain the juice, which was saved to drink. Mama would then crack the hard, hairy brown shells with a hammer (sometimes my dad did this) and pry out the white meat. Then the thin brown skin had to be peeled from each piece. The coconut pieces were hand-grated before being used for her special coconut pies and cakes. What a job!

It was quite a blessing in our family when canned flaked coconut became available. But recently I tried making this cake the old way, when Charles, my husband, and I came across fresh coconuts in the market. We had a flashback to "the good ol' days" and relived a little of our past. I can assure you that we relived that part of our past only once—that was enough!

MAKES ONE 9-INCH LAYER CAKE, SERVING 12

Butter Layer Cake
  8 tablespoons (1 stick) unsalted butter, softened,
    plus additional for the pan
  2 cups all-purpose flour, plus additional for the pan
  2½ teaspoons baking powder
  ¾ teaspoon salt
  ¾ cup milk
  1¼ teaspoons vanilla extract

1¼ cups sugar
2 large eggs

1. Preheat the oven to 375 degrees F. Grease and flour two 9-inch cake pans.
2. In a bowl, whisk together the flour, baking powder, and salt. In another bowl, combine the milk and vanilla.
3. In the bowl of an electric mixer, beat together the sugar and butter until light and fluffy. Add the eggs, one at a time, beating well after each addition. Add a third of the dry ingredients to the butter mixture and beat until just incorporated, then add half of the milk. Repeat, ending with the dry ingredients.
4. Transfer the batter to the pans, leveling the tops with a spatula. Bake until the tops of the layers are golden brown and they spring back when lightly touched at the center, about 25 minutes. Let the cakes cool on wire racks before turning them out of the pans. The layers will keep, wrapped in plastic wrap, for up to 2 days.

Fluffy Frosting
2 large egg whites
1½ cups sugar
2 teaspoons corn syrup
¼ teaspoon cream of tartar
Pinch of salt
½ teaspoon vanilla extract
1½ cups sweetened coconut flakes, preferably canned

1. Fill the bottom of a double boiler (or use a pot with a metal bowl suspended over it) with about 2 inches of water and bring it to a boil. Using a handheld electric mixer or a whisk, combine the egg whites, sugar, ½ cup water, the corn syrup, cream of tartar, and salt in the top of the double boiler. Beat the mixture on high over the boiling water until it is fluffy and forms soft peaks, about 7 minutes. Take the frosting off the heat, add the vanilla, and beat for another minute or two until cool.
2. Place one layer of cake on a serving platter and spread the top with about a third of the frosting. Scatter about ⅓ cup of the coconut over the frosting, then place the second layer of cake on top. Frost the top and sides of the cake with the remaining frosting. Scatter the remaining coconut over the cake, cupping your hands to press the coconut onto the sides. This cake is best eaten the same day it's made. Leftovers will keep for a few days, loosely covered with plastic wrap or in a sealed cake carrier.

Aunt Brenda's Homemade Peach Ice Cream

My aunt Brenda made ice cream for us in the summertime when we came over to help get the corn and peas out of my grandparents' field. We'd do some work, then have a fish- or chicken-fry for lunch outside. When the day was at its hottest, we'd all sit on the porch in the shade and shell peas or shuck corn while the breeze cooled us down. Then Brenda would serve up her peach ice cream in brown plastic square bowls with mismatched spoons. It's the best ice cream ever and now I don't have to harvest peas to get it—all I have to do is whip some up. It's very easy.

⊹ *Mom Says:* My sister, Brenda, always says, the riper the peaches, the better the ice cream. The peaches from Ruston, Louisiana, are known for their quality and taste. It's a town in the northern part of the state and is only about thirty miles from West Monroe, where Brenda lives. Therefore she gets great home-grown peaches every summer, and summer just isn't summer without fresh peach ice cream. She always tells me about it when she makes it. Of course, I'm two hours away and can only imagine I'm eating a bowl.

MAKES 2 QUARTS

2 cups (6 to 8 peaches) peeled and finely chopped ripe peaches
  (see Peeling Peaches, page 251)
½ cup sugar
1 pint half-and-half
⅛ teaspoon almond extract
1 (14-ounce) can sweetened condensed milk, or to taste

1. In a bowl, toss the peaches with the sugar, then let sit for 5 minutes.
2. Add the half-and-half and almond extract, then add the condensed milk to taste (if your peaches are very sweet and juicy, you may want to use a little less than the whole can).

3. Transfer the mixture to an ice cream machine and freeze according to the manufacturer's directions. Store the ice cream in an airtight container in the freezer for up to a week.

PEELING PEACHES

To peel peaches, bring a pot of water to a boil. Score an X in the peach skins, then dunk them in the boiling water for 30 seconds to 1 minute. Remove them from the water with a slotted spoon, let cool for a minute, then slip off their skins, using a paring knife if they are not quite loose in parts—careful, peeled peaches are slippery! The same technique can be used to peel tomatoes, too.

Sweet Summer Melon-Mint Salad

It's always nice to end a meal on a sweet note, and on hot summer evenings I crave chilled juicy melons. Fruit salads are also a great finale to a multicourse dinner party, since most people appreciate a light and refreshing dessert after a hearty meal.

SERVES 6

1 cantaloupe, seeded and cut into bite-sized chunks
3 pounds seedless watermelon, cut into bite-sized chunks
⅓ cup shredded fresh mint, plus sprigs for garnish
2 tablespoons freshly squeezed lemon juice (from 1 lemon)
2 tablespoons honey

1. Place the melon chunks and mint in a large plastic container. In a small bowl, whisk together the lemon juice and honey and drizzle it over the melon-mint mixture. Cover the container and gently shake it up and down, turning it from side to side. Alternatively, you can toss the salad with two wooden spoons.
2. Chill the salad for 30 minutes or overnight. Serve it garnished with mint sprigs.

CHAPTER 10

Preserves, Pickles, and Seasonings

Canning in the Kitchen

I was surrounded by canning and preserving when I was growing up, and I guess I took for granted all the labor involved. I do remember my mother sighing a lot and rolling her eyes when she spoke about putting stuff up—it was a lot of hot work in the summer to sterilize and process the jars. Except for some of the pickles, most of the food we put up had to be hot when it was canned, which really steamed up the kitchen. The fruits my mother and grandmother used for jellies and jams were typically all wild, like dewberries, blackberries, huckleberries, and mayhaws. With our tomato harvest from the garden we'd put up stewed tomatoes—my mom would scald them in boiling water until the skins started to crack and then she'd peel and can them. It was so nice to have them around all winter long!

Canning isn't something I do often at home in L.A., but it's nice to know that when I do want to put something up, like a great harvest of berries from the garden or a gift of mayhaw juice from my mom, I have her directions to rely on. They've never failed me and they won't fail you.

CANNING INSTRUCTIONS

Look in the canning section of your grocery or kitchen supply store for packaged jars and lids and such tools as a jar holder and canning funnel to protect hands from hot liquid. Jars should be glass Mason-type with metal lids and screw bands. You can reuse empty jars, but never try to reuse lids. Buy new ones separately.

1. Wash jars and lids thoroughly in hot soapy water.
2. Place the jars in a large pot of water fitted with a rack or steamer insert, making sure the water covers the jars completely. Cover and boil for 10 minutes. Keep the jars in the hot water until you are ready to fill them.
3. Place the lids in a bowl and pour simmering water over them. Do not boil the lids, or the seals may be ruined.
4. Fill each hot sterilized jar to within ½ inch of the top. Always wipe any residue from jar rims with a damp paper towel before placing lids on top to make sure the jars seal properly. Place the hot lids on top of each jar. Fit a clean jar ring on each jar and screw it on loosely.
5. Return the water in the pot fitted with the rack or steamer insert to a rolling boil. Use tongs to carefully place the jars in the pot, making sure the water covers the jars by at least 2 inches. Process (boil) for the time indicated in the specific recipe.
6. Remove the jars with tongs and set aside to cool. As the jars seal a pop can be heard. Successful seals will not give at all when pressed with your finger from the top. If one jar happens not to seal, place it in the refrigerator and use it first.
7. Write the date on your jar lids and use your canned goods within a year for best taste. Sealed jars should be stored in a cool, dark, and dry spot.

Bernice's Bread and Butter Pickles

My grandpa Dewey Ford was the big pickle man in the family. He was always really proud of his cucumbers—he grew long skinny ones with tiny seeds. In July, they'd come in like crazy and we'd have too many. We had to give them away, put them up, or eat them so they wouldn't go bad. And we just couldn't get them put up fast enough.

Grandma Bernice made great pickle relish, and also liked to make sweet, tangy bread and butter pickles, while Grandma Cora preferred dills. Grandma Bernice would take days to make her pickles, soaking them down and salting them. My mom made sweet pickles like Grandma Bernice, but with more turmeric, so they were yellow. Everybody did her pickles differently, with her own ingredients and techniques, like cutting the cucumber into long spears or flat, ruffled slices—the differences were subtle, but you could see them. I like these crunchy sweet pickles in sandwiches, or chopped up in salads. If you chop them fine enough they're a great stand-in for pickle relish. These pickles are ready to eat as soon as they cool down.

MAKES 2 QUARTS OR 4 PINTS

8 Kirby or Japanese cucumbers (or your choice),
    $\frac{1}{8}$ inch of blossom end cut off, sliced $\frac{1}{8}$ inch thick (about 8 cups)
3 small onions, quartered and sliced thin
$\frac{1}{4}$ cup kosher or coarse sea salt (don't use fine salt)
3 cups sugar
$2\frac{1}{2}$ cups white vinegar
1 teaspoon turmeric
1 teaspoon pickling spice

1. Combine the cucumbers, onions, and salt in a large stainless steel or glass bowl. Cover with ice cubes and let sit for 3 hours. Drain the brine that forms in the bowl along with any remaining ice cubes.
2. In a large pot, combine the sugar, vinegar, turmeric, and pickling spice and bring to a boil. Add the cucumbers and onions, return to a boil, and cook for about 2 minutes, just until the cucumbers turn from bright green to olive green.
3. Transfer the mixture to the sterilized jars, and process for 10 minutes following the directions on page 255, or let cool and refrigerate for up to 1 month.

Mom's Dill Pickles

Everyone flavors her pickles differently and I like my mom's the best. She leaves in the pretty flecks of dill and they are so light and tasty you can just sit down and eat them like a vegetable. Chill these before serving to improve their crispness.

✿ **Mom Says:** Using the right kind of cucumbers is important here—you want to look for small thin-skinned ones that don't have too many seeds. You can generally find small Kirby or Japanese cucumbers in the grocery store; both work wonderfully. When slicing the cucumbers into spears, make sure that their height is an inch shorter than the top of your jars. If you need to, you can trim the tops of the cucumbers, slice them into rounds, and stick them in along with the spears.

MAKES 8 PINTS

> 10 Kirby or Japanese cucumbers (or your choice),
>   1/8 inch of blossom end cut off, and quartered lengthwise
> 1 red bell pepper, diced
> 1 bunch fresh dill
> 8 garlic cloves, slivered
> 2 cups white vinegar
> 5 tablespoons kosher or coarse sea salt (don't use fine salt)
> 2 teaspoons dill seed
> 1 teaspoon turmeric

1. Divide the cucumber spears, bell pepper, dill, and garlic among sterilized (see page 255) pint jars and pack them in tightly. Set the filled jars aside.
2. In a medium saucepan, combine 6 cups water, the vinegar, salt, dill seed, and turmeric. Bring up to a rolling boil, then turn off the heat.
3. Pour the liquid into the jars, making sure it covers the tops of the cucumbers by about 1/2 inch, and process for 10 minutes following the directions on page 255, or let cool and refrigerate for up to 1 month.
4. Let the pickles sit for about 3 days before eating, until they cure in the brine. The longer they sit, the more dilly they become.

Blackberry Picking

When I was little, I'd go blackberry picking with my parents on Friday evenings in late spring and early summer. Blackberries were a prized possession and you usually suffered to get them. The worst part was the bugs, especially the chiggers. They're awful and get right under your skin. One time, when I was four or five years old, I sat down on a river-bank while Grandma and Grandpa Walker were busy picking berries. Well, let's just say that by the time my grandma caught me, I was covered. When we got home, my grandma bathed me in turpentine and coated me from head to toe with calamine lotion.

To protect against chiggers and thorns, you have to go into the woods all dressed up with long sleeves and big rubber boots, even though it's hot. But you can't wear gloves because if you do you can't get the berries, so your fingers suffer thorny brambles. You come out of the woods with your hands scratched up and stained pink and purple. It seems like an awful lot of trouble, but in Louisiana, where the berries are wild and free, people will go through anything because they're just so good!

Blackberry Syrup and Blackberry Jam

As kids, we helped my parents do everything in the garden and kitchen; it was part of growing up. We'd help wash berries in a big washtub and pick the little stems off. Then my mom would make her jams and jellies. She'd also pack some of the berries with sugar and freeze them for making blackberry cobbler later. I remember watching my mother get the canning jars ready. She always said, "Now come here and watch, I'm not going to be around forever, you need to learn how to do this." Well, now I've got it all written down!

❧ *Mom Says:* It's just as easy, if you are going to the trouble of it, to make jam and syrup at the same time. I always do, and am glad to have both on hand; jam for spreading on piping hot biscuits and syrup for pouring on top of blackberry pancakes (page 189). If you don't have fresh blackberries, use frozen. If you're making syrup for immediate consumption, simply place a square of plastic wrap directly on top to prevent a skin from forming over the top while you prepare the pancakes. If you are canning the syrup and jam, you might want to double or triple the recipe while you're at it.

MAKES 1⅓ CUPS SYRUP AND 1¼ CUPS JAM

> 2½ cups fresh or frozen blackberries
> 2¼ cups sugar
> ¼ cup light corn syrup

1. Combine the blackberries with 2½ cups water in a saucepan and bring to a medium simmer. Simmer for 15 minutes.
2. Strain 1 cup juice from the berries and transfer it to another saucepan for the syrup. Return the remaining berries and juice to the original saucepan for the jam. Set aside for a moment.
3. To make the syrup, add 1¼ cups of the sugar and the corn syrup to the blackberry juice.
4. Bring the syrup to a bare simmer over medium heat, stirring constantly. Keep stirring and cooking for about 8 minutes, until the syrup thickens. Either ladle the syrup into

a hot sterilized ½-pint jar (fill the jar and then store the excess in the refrigerator and use it within a month), and process for 5 minutes following the directions on page 255. Or let the syrup cool and refrigerate for up to 1 month. You can also serve it with blackberry pancakes immediately after cooking, while still warm.

5. To make the jam, add the remaining cup sugar to the cooked berries and remaining syrup. Cook over medium-high heat, stirring constantly for 8 to 10 minutes, until the mixture thickens. Either ladle the jam into a hot sterilized ½-pint jar (fill the jar and then store the excess in the refrigerator and use it within a month) and process for 10 minutes according to the directions on page 255. Or let the jam cool and refrigerate it for up to 1 month.

Old-Fashioned Watermelon Rind Preserves

✧ Mom Says: This is an old recipe handed down from my mother's mother. I have never been able to buy watermelon rind preserves like these. The ones I have found are usually sour. Ours are not pickled, but made into a sweet syrupy preserve. My sister and I loved them, but couldn't find a recipe. It was in my mother's "brain file" and she never found it necessary to write it down. My sister, Brenda, tried to make them once and it was such a mess that she said that she would never try again. I have kept trying and finally came up with preserves that come quite close to our mother's. This recipe takes some time, but the result is a sweet, delicately flavored preserve that's delicious spread on fresh biscuits or toast.

MAKES ABOUT 3 CUPS

> 8 pounds watermelon, rinsed, flesh removed, and rind peeled and
>   cut into ½-inch cubes (to yield 8 cups rind)
> Zest of ½ lemon, sliced very thin
> 2½ cups sugar
> Pinch of salt

1. In a large pot, combine the watermelon rind cubes, lemon zest, sugar, and salt and mix together. Cover and set aside for about 1 hour, until the sugar melts and juice forms.
2. Place the pot, covered, over medium heat and cook at a slow bubble for about 2 hours. Check and stir down every 20 minutes or so, pushing the top cubes down into the syrup. Reduce the heat further if the mixture tries to boil over. The rinds will darken and a medium-thick syrup will form. Test for softness from time to time as the volume reduces. They are ready when the rinds are translucent and the syrup is thick enough to coat a spoon.
3. Either ladle the preserves into three sterilized ½-pint jars and process them for 10 minutes according to the directions on page 255, or let cool and refrigerate for up to 1 month.

About Mayhaws

Mayhaws are small, round, rosy-red to slightly orange-red fruits that grow on the thorny hawthorn tree. They look a little like tiny cherries. The name mayhaw comes from the fact they they're typically ripe and ready for picking in early May. Mayhaws are native to Louisiana and grow wild in the lowlands—along shady river bottoms and swamps. Years ago, many Louisiana families like ours would make mayhaw picking an annual event. When we went out to gather mayhaws, my dad would spread an old sheet under the tree and give the trunk a mighty shake and all the ripe mayhaws would fall. Some old-timers may recall scooping up the mayhaws with a bucket as the little berries floated down streams or bogs. Now, development has made mayhaws much harder to find in the wild.

Mayhaws have been a Southern secret for years, but are now an up-and-coming industry. They are grown in commercial orchards and mayhaw jelly, mayhaw syrup, and even mayhaw wine are all being produced.

If you are fortunate enough to have access to fresh mayhaws, extract their juice yourself to make jelly. To get the juice, use 1 gallon of mayhaws, sorted and washed. Cover with water by an inch and boil until the mayhaws lose most of their red color. Strain the juice through a colander and then through clean, damp cheesecloth or jelly cloth. Refrigerate the juice for up to 2 days until ready to use. Freeze any unused juice in recipe-sized containers to use throughout the year. The juice will be tart and red and can be weakened by mixing 2 parts juice to 2 parts water. When the berries were really ripe and full of flavor, Grandma Bernice weakened hers by about 2 cups juice to 3 cups water. If you don't have access to the fresh fruit, you can mail-order mayhaw juice (see Sources, page 267).

Maw Maw Ford's Mayhaw Jelly

✧ *Mom Says:* My mother-in-law Bernice Ford made the most wonderful mayhaw jelly and I have never found a recipe for it in any cookbook. It had a lovely pale rose color and a mellow, sweet taste. Now that she is gone, when I make mayhaw jelly I think of her and wonder if she is giving her guidance and approval.

MAKES ABOUT 5 CUPS

> 4 cups mayhaw juice (see page 262 and Sources, page 267)
> 4½ cups sugar
> 1 (1¾-ounce) package pectin

1. Pour the juice into a large pot over high heat. Bring to a rolling boil and add the sugar and pectin. Stir constantly until the sugar and pectin dissolve and the mixture comes to a rolling boil that cannot be stirred down. Boil for 1 minute.
2. Take the pot off the heat and skim off the foam. Ladle the liquid immediately into five sterilized ½-pint jars, and process for 5 minutes following the directions on page 255, or let cool and refrigerate for up to 1 month.

Maw Maw Ford's Mayhaw Syrup

Grandma Bernice didn't have a separate mayhaw syrup recipe, but she would cook some of her batches of mayhaw jelly less, so that it was thin enough to pour over her delicious buttermilk biscuits. This recipe is a little different in that it's meant as syrup, so instead of pectin, we use corn syrup. Other than biscuits, try pouring it over frozen yogurt or even pancakes. You'll want to find plenty of uses for it. It's got the prettiest pink color.

MAKES ABOUT 5 CUPS

> 4 cups mayhaw juice (see page 262 and Sources, page 267)
> 4 cups sugar
> ½ cup light corn syrup

1. Place the mayhaw juice, sugar, and corn syrup in a large saucepan and bring to rolling boil that cannot be stirred down. Continue to boil, stirring, for 7 to 8 minutes, until the syrup thickens enough to coat the back of a wooden spoon.
2. Ladle the hot syrup into 5 sterilized ½-pint jars, and process for 5 minutes, following the directions on page 255 or let cool slightly and use immediately, or let cool and refrigerate for up to 1 month.

Fig Preserves

Lots of people in the South have fig trees in their yards—they grow very well in that climate. Even now, each summer we make sweet, syrupy preserves from the fruit we harvest from my grandma Cora's old fig tree. We spoon them onto steamy hot biscuits (page 191), which is a very typical Louisiana treat, or bake them into a buttermilk Bundt cake (page 244). This simple recipe can be multiplied according to how many figs you'd like to preserve.

MAKES ABOUT 8 PINTS

> 1 gallon firm fresh figs
> ¼ cup baking soda to each gallon of water for soaking figs
> 4 to 5 pounds sugar
> 1 lemon, sliced to prevent darkening, optional

1. Place the figs in a large bowl. Using ¼ cup baking soda to each gallon of water, mix enough baking soda and water to cover the figs by 2 inches. Soak for 15 to 30 minutes. Remove the figs to a colander and rinse with cold tap water.

2. Layer the figs in a heavy-bottomed stainless steel pan, followed by a layer of sugar and 1 or 2 slices lemon. Repeat the layering, completing the process with a layer of sugar on top. Refrigerate overnight to allow the sugar to form a syrup. Do not add water.

3. In the morning, place on the stove on medium-high heat until the syrup starts to bubble, then reduce to a very low simmer and cook for 4 to 5 hours. Every 20 to 30 minutes, press the floating figs gently down into the syrup and baste them with syrup that fills the spoon. *Do not stir.* The trick is not to break the tender skins. The syrup will thicken and turn amber brown.

4. Ladle the figs and the syrup immediately into sterilized pint or ½-pint jars and process for 10 minutes following the directions on page 255, or let cool and refrigerate for up to 1 month.

Faith's Special Seasoning

This is an intense, all-purpose mix of herbs and spices that kicks up the flavor of whatever you use it in. Made with paprika, onion, garlic, and cayenne pepper, it's got a bit of a Cajun feel to it. I sprinkle it on nearly everything, from vegetables and fish to poultry and meat. You can also add fresh or dried herbs to the basic mix if you want. Dill is great for fish, while marjoram and tarragon are better for poultry, and sage is a natural with pork. After you gussy up the basic mix with different herbs, you'll never recognize that it started out with the same seasonings. And mixing up a batch to keep on hand makes life so much easier!

MAKES ABOUT ½ CUP

3 tablespoons sweet paprika
2 tablespoons salt
1 tablespoon black pepper
1 tablespoon garlic powder, optional
2 teaspoons onion powder, optional
1 teaspoon dried oregano, crushed
½ teaspoon white pepper
½ teaspoon cayenne pepper
½ teaspoon dried thyme

Combine all the ingredients. Store the seasoning in an airtight jar for up to 6 months.

Sources

Comeaux's Inc.
Kaliste Saloom Store
2807 Kaliste Saloom Road
Lafayette, LA 70508
1-337-988-0516
www.comeaux.com
Andouille, tasso, Cajun seasonings, crab boil, filé, cane syrup

Jacob's World Famous Andouille
505 West Airline Highway
LaPlace, LA 70068
1-985-652-9080
1-877-215-7589
Original@JacobsAndouille.com
www.cajunsausage.com
Andouille, turkey tasso, smoked turkey wings, filé, dried beans

CajunGrocer.com
Corporate Office
208 W. Pinhook Rd.
Lafayette, LA 70503
1-888-272-9347
support@cajungrocer.com
Liquid smoke

Springhill Jellies and Syrups
Grant Fruit Processing
Pollock, LA 71467
1-866-765-2230
www.grantfruit.com
Mayhaw products

Pleasant Acres Jellies and Jams
2027 Hwy. 454
Pineville, LA 71360
1-318-253-5109
1-888-738-5109
www.jelliesandjams.com
Dried and frozen beans, mayhaw products

Day's Southern Pecan Company
727 MacArthur Drive
Alexandria, LA 71303
1-318-445-2218
1-318-442-0206
Pecans

Fogelman Pecan Farm
P.O. Box 520
Colfax, LA 71417
1-318-627-3300
alvinsales@aol.com
Pecans

Index

balsamic vinegar (*cont.*)

Pleasingly Purple Cabbage Salad with Basil Balsamic Dressing, 39

bananas

Banana Cream Pie, 231

Blueberry Brain Shake, 209

Mom's Banana-Walnut Bread, 206–207

barbecue sauce, Faith's Chicken with Barbecue Salsa, 104–105

basil

Artichoke-Parmesan Dip, 7

Cajun Grilled Vegetable Salad, 43

Faith's Fresh Petite Pea Salad, 45

Herb-and-Parmesan-Stuffed Turkey Burgers on Toasted Garlic Buns, 120–121

Homespun Basil Hummus, 18

Old-Fashioned Smothered Chicken, 106–107

Pleasingly Purple Cabbage Salad with Basil Balsamic Dressing, 39

Warm Black-Eyed Pea Salad, 46

beans, dried

Mama's Vegetable Beef Soup, 64–65

Red Beans and Rice with Andouille, 70–71

Spicy Chicken Soup with Fresh Green Chiles, 56–57

See also black-eyed peas

beef

Fried Mini Meat Pies, 24–25

Golden Brown Beef Stew, 126–127

Juicy Beef Pot Roast, 134–135

Mama's Vegetable Beef Soup, 64–65

Mom's Smoky Beef Brisket, 130–131

Mom's Stuffed Cabbage Rolls with Sweet Cabbage Sauté, 146–148

Rest of the Post Roast Po' Boys, 12–13

Smothered Steak with Onion Gravy, 132–133

Spicy Beef Stew with Vegetables and Tomatoes, 128–129

"Student Union" Burger on the Griddle, 144–145

Tiny Meat Loaf for Two, 142–143

bell peppers. *See* peppers, bell

Bernice's Bread and Butter Pickles, 256

Bernice's English Pea Salad, 44

The Best Pie Crust, 222–223

beverages

Blueberry Brain Shake, 209

Chocolate Coffee, 207

Fresh Mint Iced Tea, 210

Peaches-n-Creamy Shake, 208

Big-Time Brownies, 212–213

biscuits

Buttermilk Biscuits, 192

Cheese Biscuits, 192

Cinnamon Raisin Biscuits, 192–193

Cream Cheese and Chive Biscuits, 194

Granola Biscuits, 195

Homey Pot Pies, 116–117

Mom's Angel Biscuits, 196–197

Mom's Blackberry Cobbler with Biscuit Topping, 220–221

Sausage Surprise Biscuits, 193

Skillet Drop Biscuits with Variations, 191–193

black beans, Spicy Chicken Soup with Fresh Green Chiles, 56–57

blackberries

Blackberry Jam, 259–260

Blackberry Pancakes with Blackberry Syrup, 189

Blackberry Syrup, 259–260

Mom's Blackberry Cobbler with Biscuit Topping, 220–221

tips for picking, 258

black-eyed peas

Black-Eye Pea Soup with Sausage and Mustard Greens, 61

Red-Hot Black-Eyed Peas, 158

Warm Black-Eyed Pea Salad, 46

Warm Pasta Salad with Chicken Andouille Sausage, Mustard Greens, and Black-Eyed Peas, 48–49

blueberries

Blueberry Brain Shake, 209

Pint-Sized Blueberry Pie, 226–227

bran, Peach-Pecan Bran Muffins, 204–205